D1453371

SEAN LALLY

THE AIR
FROM OTHER
PLANETS

A BRIEF HISTORY
OF ARCHITECTURE
TO COME

Lars Müller Publishers

"*There is one profession and only one, namely architecture, in which progress is not considered necessary, where laziness is enthroned, and in which the reference is always yesterday.*"

Le Corbusier, *Towards a New Architecture* (1923)

"*You know, they say three species disappear off the planet every day. You wonder how many new ones are being created.*"

Fox Mulder (David Duchovny), "The Host," *The X-Files*, season 2, episode 2

"*Alice laughed. 'There's no use trying,' she said. 'One can't believe impossible things.'*

"'*I dare say you haven't had much practice,' said the Queen. 'When I was your age, I always did it for half an hour a day. Why, sometimes I've believed as many as six impossible things before breakfast.'*"

Lewis Carroll, *Through the Looking Glass*, Chapter 5 (1865)

8   Introduction
    NOSTALGIC FOR THE FUTURE

40 AMPLIFICATION

94 MATERIAL ENERGIES

154 SENSORIAL ENVELOPES

200 THE SHAPE OF ENERGY

243 Appendix

NOSTALGIC
FOR THE FUTURE

The architect is not so different from the traditional image of an explorer, someone who sets out to discover new geographic territories never before documented and experienced. For explorers, discovery might require traveling great distances, heights, or depths to physically place themselves somewhere that previously may have been only observed from very far away (outer space) or imagined to exist from technological conjecture (ocean depths). In doing so, new human perspective and knowledge is created, changing our relationship to both this new location as well as our initial presumptions about the places we left before our expedition. These explorations are as much a reorientation and rereading of our starting points as they are a discovery of new places that only a few may experience directly. Architects operate within a similar framework; unlike explorers, however, they don't need to travel great distances to see landscapes shift and change underneath their feet. Architects do this by standing still and pushing environments prematurely into time, altering the world's physical makeup and advancing it into the future. They call for qualities and conditions not seen in the world before. Recognizing the elastic nature of the environment around us, the architect does not physically trek to find scientific truths and define geographic certainties, but instead induces the *potential futures* layered within the existing environments that others would assume they already know.

These potential futures of the environments already around us are within our purview and no less obtainable than the summits yet unclimbed or the remote territories still waiting to be traversed for the first time. The distance that an architect travels isn't calculated in miles or altitude, but in time. This is because the world we know can never be maintained in permanent stasis. Everything must move, and how one chooses to move with the temporal world is what separates us from one another. Some architects work diligently to reproduce a previous moment in time—maybe one they once belonged to or wished they had—preserving a particular instance for as long as physically possible. Others would say that they absorb the "now," a pause within this particular moment that is to be appreciated and exploited within a given exploration. Still others would say that the present speaks less to them than do the potential futures mapped out in their minds. As Fredric Jameson has said, these individuals have never really seen the ground they move upon, but "only their own faces," projected and embedded in the landscapes before them, yet to be realized.[1] The last are our architectural explorers, and the discrete pockets they design within a much larger landscape along Earth's surface serve as "mock futures." These architects' greatest contribution isn't necessarily to attempt to imagine the real future, but instead to "transform our own present into the determinate past of something yet to come."[2] The point of this transformation is not simply to keep such a future alive in our imaginations; it is actually to demonstrate the shortcomings currently before us that in reality obstruct that future's development.[3] This book is therefore as much about our actions today as it would appear to be about the long distances stretched out ahead of us.

As architects (as explorers), how aggressive have we been in our "travels" to seek out new frontiers and territories? Are we continuing to make small incremental trips around the outskirts of places we've already been, or do we need to travel still further and set our sights on the design of environments and spaces yet unseen? As ambitious as architects have been in the past in developing these mock futures, architecture has actually refrained from engaging a range of materials so ubiquitous and commonly shared that they have been largely dismissed. Until architects take on these ignored building materials for making the spaces and places we require, the outer edges of the profession and its spatial and aesthetic capabilities will remain unexplored.

ARCHITECTURE OF ENERGIES

Architecture is much more than the building of an object on a site: it is a reinvention of the site itself. The microclimates of internal heating and cooling, outdoor shadows and artificial lighting, vegetation, the importation of building materials, and the new activities that will occur there create new places in time

EXPLORATION OF NEW GROUNDS
Sir Edmund Hillary and Tenzing Norgay, the first climbers confirmed to have reached the summit of Mount Everest on May 29, 1953.

on-site. To construct such places, architects often seek to design walls between activities and spaces, as they have done for thousands of years. The image in our mind of such a "building" consists of walls that are used to define a space's perimeter, standing there to protect what lies on one side of those walls from the climatic and environmental context on the other side. It is difficult to overstate just how much both the architect and the people who use a building's spaces rely on walls and surfaces to define what we refer to as architecture. Sketching with lines, making models with blocks, and then realizing those representations with solid masses of steel, stone, wood, and concrete is our fundamental method of operation. Producing representations of walls and surfaces is now assumed to be the defining act of architectural design. These solid masses of materials separate and divide one space from another, absorbing our aesthetic and cultural values in the resultant forms they take. The use of a surface to mediate between existing weather and the activities, people, or objects on the other side can firmly be identified as the longest-running strategy for defining space in architecture—from the caves used by early humans and a civilization's first primitive huts to the tallest, most recent skyscrapers. Yet today architects often strive to make those very walls thinner and more transparent, so that in the right light and at the right angle, they momentarily disappear from view. This points to an unquestionably strong desire in the profession to remove or move past its reliance on these surfaces. Architects have just been unsure how best to do so, because when this does happen, the strategies in place for how we organize activities and define physical boundaries in an environmental context will be fundamentally rewritten.

Other types of spaces and boundaries exist that are represented not by a single line but instead through gradients of energy intensities nested within their surroundings. These are the particles, waves, and chemical interactions of energy that continually surround us, yet are dismissively lumped together and referred to as "air." We recognize this type of gradient space in the oasis—a pocket of moisture, vegetation, and vivid colors set against a backdrop of monotone sand—or in the image of thousands of pinwheel galaxies clustered together and juxtaposed against a black background of deep space. These shapes and spaces don't exist as bounded, walled-off entities, but as localized, concentrated exceptions to the surroundings they nest within. They stand apart and provide a resource of relief or opportunity not available in their immediate context. The boundaries that make these microclimates and ecosystems distinct from their surrounding

NEW WORLD
FARMING
Still from *The Hitchhiker's Guide to the Galaxy* (2005).

context and each other are shifting and potentially even invisible to the human eye; they require alternate sensory perceptions to perceive them as they intensify and ebb, seeking equilibrium.

Instead of thinking of architecture as a mass of inert and ossified energy—even stone and steel were not always solid masses—standing as walls in opposition to their surroundings and carving out interior space, why not look to intensify those very energy systems we know are capable of creating microclimates and distinct ecosystems so as to make them architectural materials themselves? This process is more than just replacing one material with another. These intensified pockets of energy will also become new methods for organizing the activities and events of our domestic and public lives, informing social interactions in a manner not seen in the effects exerted today by surface architecture. Such a fundamental shift will question the standards we've come to take for granted when qualifying architectural shape, how the human body interacts and identifies with those boundary shapes, and how those variables trickle down to affect our interactions with each other.

One of architecture's primary acts is to define the spatial boundaries that organize and hold specified activities within them. The behavioral properties of the materials used to make that boundary not only influence the physical characteristics of that space (maximum height, span, aperture sizes), but also determine how the human body perceives and senses those boundary changes (opacity, transparency, acoustics), which then informs the behaviors and movements of the individuals using the space. This definition of boundaries is one that architects have continually tested and subverted as new materials, construction methods, and social trends have emerged over the centuries. It follows that if energy could be controlled and deployed as physical boundaries that define and organize spaces the human body can detect and recognize, wouldn't that be architecture? These new building materials would only need to demonstrate that they could absorb the "responsibilities" of boundaries—able to determine spatial hierarchies, provide security, hold aesthetic value, etc.—for them to be called architecture. Current trends just on the periphery of the discipline that could make this a possibility only need to be integrated through the lens of the architect to see their potential.

The three statements below identify opportunities drawn from tangent streams of inquiry that together, in their overlap, highlight a position on using material energies that architects would appear prime to engage. They bridge the two most quickly advancing areas of research standing just at the periphery of the architectural profession: energy and bioengineering.

Current advances in how various forms of energy (electromagnetic, thermodynamic, acoustic, and chemical) are controlled and visualized are giving architects a new set of materials for constructing the physical boundaries that define space. These material energies *create gradient boundaries of intensities inherent to the two basic properties of energy (particles and waves). This is a fundamental shift away from the physical boundaries made of surfaces and geometries that architecture is most familiar with.*

Chemical performance enhancers, implants and surgeries are artificially altering the human body's physiology and means of sensory perception. These alterations permit the human body to perceive a range of material energies and potential systems of organization that were previously imperceptible and hence under-utilized for constructing physical boundaries in architecture.

At the intersection of these two seemingly distinct areas of research—increased control and deployment of material energies to define geographic boundaries, and increased sensory sensitivity of the human body to detect and recognize those edges—lie new potentials for architecture. The unique properties of material energies, coupled with how the spaces they define are calibrated to the body, offer the possibility for unique architectural shapes, spatial typologies, organizational hierarchies, and aesthetic values.

The specific opportunity that this project seeks to explore comes from the interconnectivity, and at times seemingly a convergence, of interrelated feedback between these two advancing areas of investigation. If architects, whose role is to define physical boundaries between people and activities, can demonstrate the spatial and social ramifications that come from the human body's interacting and sensing a new set of boundary types, the implications could be immense. The scope of this shift includes impacts on the building industries and technology fields that supply materials, the social activities and interactions between people using spaces, the associated aesthetic values when architecture builds with these materials, and the eco-politics and policies affected within this greater directive. In identifying these tangent streams, the goal is not to point outside of the architectural profession to identify something that is missing, but instead to highlight threads coursing through architecture now that only need to be followed for these new developments to be taken to their full advantage. Architecture can do more than borrow from outside directives: it can be involved in propelling both of these two areas of research further, intertwining them into the daily lifestyles of our cultures by demonstrating that a new use of material energies coupled with an improved potential to perceive and sense them produces more than the sum of the two.

SHIFTS IN THINKING

The Earth receives one billionth of the sun's energy, and as inhabitants of Earth, we currently utilize about one millionth of that one billionth.[4] As small a number as this may appear to be, keep in mind that for the several thousand years that we've recorded our manipulations and designs on the Earth's surface, it has only been in a remarkably short period of time that we have gone from only harnessing fossil fuels to pursuing hydropower, nuclear power, and solar energy collection. Today we assemble stone to construct a building because the energy required to quarry, ship, stack, and sustain it is thought to be economically feasible and compatible with our daily capabilities. But just over a hundred years ago, we didn't have the technological knowledge of mechanical systems to create the climate of San Diego inside a building in Saskatchewan in February—with a specified temperature, relative humidity, and interior light level—all while pulling at least a portion of the energy required to do so from something other than a fossil fuel. But we can do that today. We can manipulate the microclimates on the exteriors of our buildings as well, through casting shadows, reflections from glazed surfaces, and excess energy dumps from mechanical systems on building roofs and from city infrastructure. However, this manipulation today is most often seen as either an unintended by-product (shadow cast from a building height) or simply the filling of an interior void with a recognizable and predefined climate. In years to come, as the amount of research on energy collection and manipulation steadily expands, opportunities will continue to grow. No longer will energy be relegated to a geological remnant, something stacked as a building's exterior (stone) or burned to heat that same building's interior (coal and oil), but instead it will be harnessed, manipulated, and designed to subsume and advance the roles we currently give walls. But to what end? Will we aim only to conduct our existing lifestyles and run our buildings more efficiently and inexpensively, or might these opportunities instead be seen as initiators for reinventing those very lifestyles and architectures?

There are many examples of such paradigm shifts in architecture, when advancements outside of architecture, along with the creative imagination of the architectural discipline and its ability to rethink current spatial definitions, have stimulated new territories of exploration. Contrary to how most people might envision such a shift (whether in science or in architecture), significant breaks with the past generally don't occur through immediate and sudden ruptures. They come about because the current, known methods of solving a particular problem either can no longer do so or fail to take advantage of new developments from outside that particular discipline. Often these shifts cannot be attributed to one individual or even a specific date and year. Instead, they occur gradually through a competition of ideas, eventually resulting in the "rejection of one previous theory or the adoption of another."[5] In architecture, the result might be the advent of a new building material (steel), or a new method of construction (prefabrication), or ways of accommodating a new set of activities that didn't exist earlier (the production of motion pictures). Advancements in these cases do more than swap one material out for another to make a process more efficient: they re-inform and influence the social and political frameworks within which individuals live.

Although it might not be necessary to go back as far as the nineteenth century to identify such a paradigm shift, the great exhibitions of England and France are an especially strong example. A combination of factors, including advancements in smelting iron, the ability to produce larger panes of glass, and the Industrial Revolution, which produced cheaper and more abundant goods—all coupled with the nationalistic pride of the countries involved in these developments—resulted in the advent of entirely new spaces and aesthetics. The Crystal Palace, Eiffel Tower, and Grand Palais at the time were unique structures of increased height, transparency, and interior spans, executed via a prefabrication strategy of construction that drastically reduced production time. However, as inspirational as they were for future projects like the railroad stations that dotted Europe and the United States half a century later, their appearance was not sudden.

These materials and techniques had first been used to duplicate previous architectural forms and typologies. Iron provided a structural strength that would first be demonstrated in bridge construction. Its cheaper production costs and increased fire resistance made it an obvious replacement for wood, yet early projects simply swapped one material for the other, unsure how to capitalize on the new material's qualities and so reimagine the resultant architecture. It was not until a combination of pressures from outside of architecture alone—including both the desire of competing nations to display the products of their Industrial Revolutions and to show off newly discovered exotic specimens from their warmer overseas colonies, which required greenhouses able to produce and maintain the necessary artificial climates—that iron's greatest potential manifested itself in the great exhibition halls of the nineteenth century. These structures in turn suggested the ever greater possibilities in exploration, ingenuity, and technological advancements for constructing in steel, prefiguring the towers and skyscrapers that later emerged. That combination of factors both within and beyond architecture produced a paradigm shift that the profession had no option but to embrace and explore if it wasn't to be left behind, stuck in an antiquated practice unable to adapt to shifting needs. These new opportunities offered architects a chance to do more than improve upon a predetermined service, as the architecture that emerged re-informed the lifestyles and spaces of the people that embraced it in unanticipated ways.

The buildings of the nineteenth century's great exhibitions demonstrate where opportunities can exist for new spatial and formal typologies to emerge, when a dialogue is encouraged between new material advancements and those broader social and economic trends that originate outside of architecture. Architecture is more than a function of practicality, and the shapes and configurations it takes are never "neutral translations of prerequisites."[6] There is a reciprocal relationship between the social forces and dynamics of our current lives (domestic norms, social etiquettes, or advancements in the speed of communication or travel) and how the materials available to architects are controlled and deployed. The dialogue between the two variables gives us the shapes of architecture's next incarnation that then fold back to influence the people and activities using them.

It is important to note that the technological breakthroughs, knowledge, and opportunities that architects reference and pull from often lie on the periphery of the discipline. Architecture has often existed in an uneasy balance, both needing to demonstrate its particular expertise to outside professions while simultaneously exhibiting its ability to speculate upon new forms in untested directions that inspire these very same outside communities. Too much of the former and architecture appears to be nothing more than a service industry; too much of the latter and the architect could be dismissed as a science fiction stage set designer.

In its pursuit of demonstrable expertise, the architectural profession has become increasingly specialized, splintering into subsets that then become separate regulated professions. Simply referring to the credits associated with any large-scale building under construction today shows just how many specialists are needed (or at least required by law) to realize the increasingly complex demands of such an architectural project. This includes licensed professionals like architects, landscape architects, planners, interior designers and structural, mechanical, electrical, and acoustical engineers. Many projects add to this the expertise of unlicensed consultants, including traffic engineers, team builders, telecommunication specialists, graphic designers, and security consultants. It was only two hundred years ago that the architect and engineer were seen as the same individual, before these roles split into two distinct professions. Today there are no fewer than seven licensed design professions that have splintered out from this original trunk, with the American Society of Interior Designers (1975) and the American Institute of Certified Planners (1978) being two of the most recent.[7]

Conversations associated with energy in architecture appear rooted in the securing of yet another professional subset: a governing body concerned with LEED (Leadership in Energy and Environmental Design) certification, which is likely to direct discussions about energy and the environment in a loop of conservation and cost-efficiency. This approach prematurely limits the discourse by tying energy's value in architecture solely to the act of conservation.[8] While this book would not argue against any one of these directives as somehow being unworthy of our efforts, it does state that if architecture wants to increase the value of the discipline, proving its value by claiming yet another territory of service and expertise is not the only option available. Just as iron was originally seen as only a cost-effective, more fire-resistant replacement for wood, but then became the means to produce new buildings of vast interior spaces and heights, architecture is now in the position to associate energy with opportunities beyond simply reproducing ideal weather conditions within the interior of buildings cheaply and efficiently.

The degree to which a society can manipulate energy, and the influence this has on that society's development, are of critical importance. This is because energy plays a pivotal role in the advancement of civilizations, both in securing the sustainability of a culture's existence and in making large strides in that culture's broader knowledge base once energy is seen as a launching pad for new explorations and not just a fuel to run current ones.

From the first campfire to steam power, electricity, and nuclear power, energy has played a pivotal role in everything from the first agricultural food production, to high speed communication and travel, to the capturing of views of deep space that reinforce speculations about the origins of the universe. Not only streamlining the lives we currently live, energy is at the epicenter of our imagination as we seek the innovation that influences artistic, technological, and social growth.

Ushering energy into this larger role requires speculation by the architect, drawing from developments beyond professional borders and transcending mere expressed expertise. These speculations on the part of architects then feed back into adjacent disciplines, supplying new inspiration and focus. This is a relationship that is familiar in the interactions of science fiction and the sciences. Science fiction provides a type of "inspiration theory" in its ability to supply "plausible, fully thought out scenarios of alternate realities in which some sort of compelling innovation has taken place."[9] Science fiction's contribution to the sciences and engineering is rooted in its ability to inspire a new generation to take on these questions and seek out professions that can contribute to the discussion. It engages the general public to become familiar with alternative opportunities before them, essentially building the audience needed to request, demand, and maybe even expect these innovations within their lifetime.

Architectural innovation in energy is currently judged by how the architect integrates technological devices that reduce energy consumption after a building or site has already been designed—not by the capacity of energy to produce the design characteristics of a building. Advancements in energy research currently focus on increasing the efficiency of the machinery that consumes energy as a fuel (air-conditioning and heating units)—not on deepening our understanding of energy as possessing a wide range of material properties (electromagnetic forces, thermodynamics, sound waves, and chemical interactions). Harnessing energy will always be a part of the equation, but in the near future it will become a much smaller portion of what determines a project's viability. The act of releasing energy, how we shape it to create intensified pockets and constellations of space ready for habitation, and the architectural roles we entrust to it as a physical material, will move to the foreground. This shift in action will turn energy from a resource into a material, and therefore into architecture—a building block for constructing space and defining organizational systems.

An often overlooked variable needed to advance technological developments associated with energy is a growing public demand that exceeds the expertise of engineers and scientists alone. People must be enticed, and their imaginations stimulated, by seeing what our lifestyles could be like if we would only embrace this potential. Today, in a time of climate change and environmental degradation, the public is faced with moralistic calls for sacrifice, but the resulting betterment of the world can seem imperceptible: individuals are rarely at a vantage point to witness the benefits of a carbon-neutral lifestyle or the safety of a protected species in its habitat. The need to make calls for change is not in dispute, but people are most willing to make changes when their actions can be oriented toward a greater vision, one that doesn't fall into a less than inspiring choice of either preventing a catastrophe or maintaining the status quo.

Today's prevailing dialogue related to the environment is rooted in the premise that if we're lucky, we'll just get to keep what we already know. But that cannot happen. Even if species stopped going extinct and the atmosphere stopped changing its chemical composition, we still would not be experiencing today the same surroundings we woke up to yesterday because nothing on Earth or anywhere else stands still. The images of our future and the environment we live in should consist of more than holding on with white knuckles to what we have because, truly, this isn't obtainable. What architects can do instead is plant in the imaginations of others the seeds of alternative and responsible lifestyles of the future.

"I HAVE SEEN THE FUTURE" — SELLING A LIFESTYLE
Futurama by Norman Bell Geddes, the General Motors Pavilion of the 1939 World's Fair.

In its pavilion at the 1939 World's Fair—called Futurama—General Motors exhibited a projected future complete with models of suburbs, motorways, and cloverleaf overpasses, a comprehensive new reality that brought people out of the cities and into the surrounding landscape by paving roadways in petroleum-based asphalt on which oil-fueled cars could travel. The designs and transportation directives implemented in Futurama by its designer Norman Bel Geddes weren't necessarily novel at the time; they had already circulated in the work of others, including Frank Lloyd Wright's 1932 Broadacre City and Le Corbusier's 1925 Voisin Plan for Paris. But Futurama gave business giants an opportunity to expose Depression-era Americans to visions and ideas lying just on the horizon.[10] The exhibition enticed the public by showing how automobile transportation could "transform both lives and landscapes" and, as a result, helped companies like General Motors and Shell get the subsidies they needed, that is, federal investments in roadways that would not only make these companies global forces but fortify our dependence on the cars and oil they produced.[11]

On the one hand, this book argues that the materiality of energy can influence and inform the spaces and shapes of architecture. On the other hand, it realizes that if great strides and investments are going to be made in how energy is harnessed and controlled, they will have to come from enticing the general public through demonstrations of new lifestyles, offering visions of a future that the public would be willing, quite frankly, to covet and to make some sacrifices to obtain. The architectural profession is in the best position to deliver the visions and mock futures needed. In offering up the opportunity to achieve these new environments and lifestyles, architecture can create public demand that will generate the necessary pressure to encourage industry to make the required leaps in technology and innovation. In return, not only will architecture gain a new set of material energies with which to build, but these pressures will impact and re-inform some of our basic assumptions about physical boundaries, spatial organizations, lifestyle, and aesthetics, both for those working within architecture and for the users that engage it. In doing so, we have to be prepared for the realization that this future might not necessarily look like the environment surrounding us today, but could very well be one we can nurture and sustain.

The book begins with the chapter "amplification," which demonstrates that architecture has elected to define its shape and spaces through devices of mediation (surfaces, walls, inert masses) that temper the energies that make up the environmental context rather than strengthening and amplifying them as defining boundaries themselves. The chapter discusses architecture's long-running interest in advancing materials for construction and the influence this has had on spaces and typologies, from the tower configurations tied to reinforced concrete and steel, to the exotic microclimates of the greenhouses associated with iron and glass. Strengthening and amplifying the energies that course through our surroundings would enable architects to develop energy as a building material in its own right. The chapter describes the environment that our bodies inhabit as a material ready for our design engagement—a site of action formed by a construction of materials that do more than produce recognized climates and can become architecture itself.

The second chapter, "Material Energies," takes a more detailed look into energy as a building material, referred to collectively as *material energies*. The chapter begins by contrasting material energies with two existing strategies of using energy already familiar to those both inside and outside the design professions: atmospheric effects and climate control. Though they exist on opposite sides of the spectrum, what ties atmospheric effects and comfort control together with material energies are their shared physical properties: waves, particles, and chemical components. What separates them from each other is the degree to which each can define and control the physical boundary needed to produce a space for a specified activity. The intention is to familiarize the reader with these compositional properties before describing what makes material energies unique, which is their potential to absorb the spatial demands placed on a material that must provide the control needed for activities, events, and whatever people and goods are involved. The chapter concludes by looking at the physical properties and proclivities of material energies through contemporary examples that point to how they perform and how they will effect an architecture that relies less on points, lines, and surfaces to shape geographic boundaries and more on gradients of intensities—the hallmark of material energies.

The third chapter, "Sensorial Envelopes," discusses the human body as a continuous calibration device central to the construction of the physical boundaries of architecture. The chapter begins with a survey of historical investigations of human anatomy and physiology; in their representation of proportion and scale, these studies had a huge impact on architectural tendencies of their times and still reverberate today. Although our knowledge of the human body has increased significantly through an array of discoveries since Leonardo da Vinci's "Vitruvian Man," the human body itself has not witnessed an actual physiological change over that time. Examples abound today, however, that illustrate the progression and increased sensitivity of our human senses. These include the development of visual aids, from glasses to contact lenses to laser eye surgery; research advancements in immunology for better understanding and correcting of imbalances and attacks on our body's immune systems; and pharmaceutical enhancements that supply psychiatric medication to our central nervous system, such as antidepressants and stimulants, and regulatory sex hormones.

The chapter makes the claim that though such developments were originally intended to help correct or heal a condition for those either who were born with a perceived deficiency or who developed an ailment during their lifespan, interventions like these will inevitably get reconstituted to enhance performance for those already considered healthy. In the very near future, these two seemingly distinct areas of research—increased sensory sensitivity and the architect's growing control over the material energy world—will eventually come into a stronger dialogue with each other. The calibration of the human body will extend beyond the proportions and ergonomics that today relate our skin to architecture's surfaces, and our bodies will instead be understood in terms of gradient *sensorial envelopes*, intertwined with the new shapes of architecture made from material energies. As the development and control of the material energies that act as stimuli for the human body intensify, the body's receptors will need heightening to interact with and perceive them. The chapter views these sensorial envelopes as a negotiation between the body's capacities of perception and the material energies that produce the architecture.

The final chapter, "The Shape of Energy," moves the discussion beyond the properties of material energies and considers what shape this architecture will take. Right now, energy takes its architectural shape from either the devices that harness it (solar panels, wind turbines), the mechanical systems that distribute and release it, or the surfaces that mediate it (shades, porches, overhangs). Rarely is the shape of the released energy itself considered. A discussion of shape in architecture might appear to be so fundamental as to not require clarification, but in actuality shape is exactly what is eluding the architect who would envision working with energy as an architectural material. By failing to give shape to the energy systems that are released from, or trapped within, these devices, we are limited to seeing architecture's most intrinsic forms only through the restrained filter of the artifacts that produce, transport, or mediate them.

In exploring the architectural shape of energy, the chapter delves into issues of variability and the tolerances of construction and assembly when architectural form takes on the same properties as the climatic variables that it will interact with. It is only by giving energy shapes, and requiring that those shapes produce conglomerations, subdivisions, and aesthetic choices, that spatial and organizational implications can be discussed. The question arises as to what these shapes are that we now recognize as defining architecture, and how the aesthetic and spatial proclivities that they exhibit inform larger organizational typologies and social experiences.

Complementing these four written chapters are fifteen "concept spreads" that illustrate some of the terminologies introduced in the chapters as well as strategies for future design implementation. The concept spreads are intended to act independently of any specific design outcome represented in the work of the design office Sean Lally WEATHERS. They were created to be porous enough for other designers to move through them, pulling ideas from them for their own work, yet strong enough to illustrate the overarching opportunities that pertain to architecture before us today.

The work of Sean Lally WEATHERS is intended to be viewed less as a direct representation of the directives within this book and more as yet another medium in which these directives have been explored. The written chapters and the examples of design projects thus are vehicles for exploring the book's ideas; they inform one another, and neither is all-inclusive. The concept spreads comprise the thread that links them together. The examples do not argue their case as being "the environmentally responsible thing to do," nor do they build up a trajectory toward a single, inevitable result by tracing or rereading an existing design genealogy. What they show is ultimately a dialogue between advancements from peripheral disciplines (including products of political and social pressures) and the intrinsic demands of architecture to organize territories, a dialogue that ultimately provides the architect with a new accepted model to operate within.[12] Fed by an interplay of conversations with predecessors, contemporaries, and "immediate successors," this project hopes to contribute to an ever-growing stockpile of knowledge, speculations, and constructs.[13]

The title of the book, *The Air from Other Planets: A Brief History of Architecture to Come*, is intended to suggest to the reader a vision of what architecture might become once it goes beyond its traditional associations. Although the book is solely concerned with architecture on Earth, the title plays off the recent and ongoing identification of dozens of Earth-like planets within just a small portion of our own galaxy by NASA's Kepler Mission.[14] The NASA mission is to find planets within the "Goldilocks" zone—planets that are close in size to Earth while existing in a habitable zone around their own stars, thus increasing the likelihood of water and the possibility of life. Each of these planets has atmospheric conditions and patterns with the potential of supporting life that we have never seen before. Given that the book is about the use of energy as a material that will expand the very definition of architecture and the environments we will eventually create, the title is intended to help launch that perception and advance our imaginings of what we can do with energy in ways that go beyond reproducing the climates and weather systems we already know.

Though the trajectory of the book may at times appear directed to a long distant goal, these ideas are not part of a game of contradictions—simply playing against what is standard today—but are instead a recognition of an exposed thread worthy of following. I wrote this book not as a historian or theoretician, but as a design architect who sees a vein of ore in the ground that I find worthy of following down, a plausible future that I seek to amplify and direct more specifically. To paraphrase Robert Venturi, this book is a projection of what seems to me true for architecture now and in the near future, rather than a diatribe against what seems false.

1 Fredric Jameson, *Archaeologies of the Future: The Desire Called Utopia and Other Science Fictions* (London: Verso, 2005), 405.

2 Ibid., 288.

3 Ibid., 288–289.

4 Michio Kaku, "Star Makers," *COSMOS* magazine, 2 November 2007. Kaku attributes this figure to Donald Goldsmith, but a direct source has not been found.

5 S. Thomas Kuhn, *The Structure of Scientific Revolutions*, 3rd ed. (Chicago and London: University of Chicago Press, 1996), 8.

6 Robin Evans, "Figures, Doors, and Passages," in *Translations from Drawing to Building and Other Essays* (Cambridge, MA: MIT Press, 1997), 56.

7 "Types of Interior Design Legislation," at Careers in Interior Design, http://www.careers-ininteriordesign.com/licensing.html (accessed 26 April 26, 2013). The regulation of licensed professionals varies from country to country as well as from state to state within the United States. As an example, twenty-five states and jurisdictions have enacted some type of interior design legislation. Of these, sixteen have title acts and six have practice acts. The professional organization and the organization that administers the licensing of that profession are often separate groups. For instance, the American Institute of Architects was formed in 1857, but the National Council of Architectural Registration Board, which controls the architectural registration process, was formed in 1919.

8 "LEED," at United States Green Building Council, http://new.usgbc.org/leed (accessed 26 April 2013).

9 Neal Stephenson, "Innovation Starvation," *World Policy Journal* (September 2011), 11–16.

10 Lawrence W. Speck, "Futurama," in *Norman Bel Geddes Designs America*, ed. Donald Albrecht (New York: Abrams, 2012), 291.

11 Speck, "Futurama," 302.

12 Kuhn, *Structure of Scientific Revolutions*, 3rd ed. (Chicago and London: The University of Chicago Press, 1996), 23.

13 Ibid., 15.

14 "Kepler: A Search for Habitable Planets," at NASA Ames Research Center, http://kepler.nasa.gov/Mission/QuickGuide/ (accessed 18 April 2013).

BEYOND MEDIATION

The use of a surface to mediate the existing energies and climates
of a site in order to provide spaces for activities, people, and
objects is without question architecture's defining characteristic.
Surfaces of mediation currently hold all the aesthetic values
and organizational controls associated with architecture. If architects stop seeing architecture as the result of mediation—a process
of blocking, absorbing, or allowing various forms of energy
inside, mainly without altering them—those same energy variables
can become the subject of design. Architecture then becomes
an act of amplification—strengthening and augmenting the
characteristics and properties of the particles and waves that both
the surrounding environment and architecture share. Amplification
means designing the material composition of the local environment that the body moves through in order to meet the spatial
and organizational needs associated with architecture. The action
is similar to introducing currents into a body of water or using
its thermoclines, those demarcations that are often sudden and
striking in their contrasts in temperature from one region of water
to another. The responsibility we currently place on surfaces
and geometries to provide architectural systems would be taken
up by the amplified energy that currently courses through the
environment, making these various forms of energy the building
blocks of architecture.

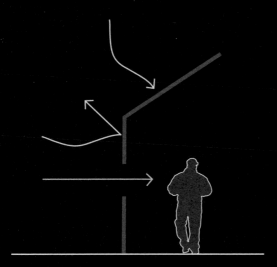

Architecture as "mediation"

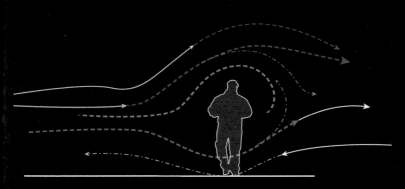

Architecture as "amplification"

35

AMPLIFICATION

Amplification is a strategy that intensifies and builds upon the existing properties of a known condition, accentuating them until the condition becomes something other than itself. Producing architecture through amplification involves strengthening the energies associated with exterior microclimates until they become a material to build with. The use of these energies is intended to go beyond simply emulating existing weather or ideal climates, as we currently do, using the conditioned energy to fill architecture's interiors. Amplification may begin with the parameters associated with climate (pressure, temperature, humidity, solar radiation, and precipitation), but it moves beyond them, augmenting and manipulating their properties as an initiator of design. Just as the building materials of concrete, steel, and glass that architects currently build with are more than a collection of existing geologic resources (lime, water, iron ore, and sand), and the buildings these materials come together to create do more than reproduce existing cave typologies, designing with our available energy systems is more than reproducing familiar climates. Instead, the architect must begin "sketching" in the units of measurement associated with energy. It's only through a better understanding of energy's characteristics and behaviors that the architect will be in a position to demand more from energy as a material to build with, giving architecture alternative definitions of boundary edges, shapes, and aesthetics.

ATMOSPHERIC VARIABLE
Electromagnetic, thermodynamic,
sound waves, and chemical compositions.

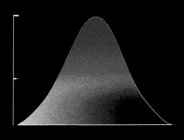

AMPLIFIED ATMOSPHERIC VARIABLE
Localized and intensified to produce architectural space.

SHAPING ENERGIES

Architecture's shape (the physical edges that control a person's movement, the spatial typologies that organize activities, and the aesthetic qualities conveyed) is created through a dialogue between the building materials used and the human body's ability to detect the boundaries those materials produce. Particles and waves of energy produce gradients of intensity, requiring the human body's sensory perception to be sensitive enough to detect and respond to the properties of those more blurred edge conditions. The shape of this architecture is a result of a precise calibration between the senses of the human body and the *material energies* that the body can perceive and come into contact with.

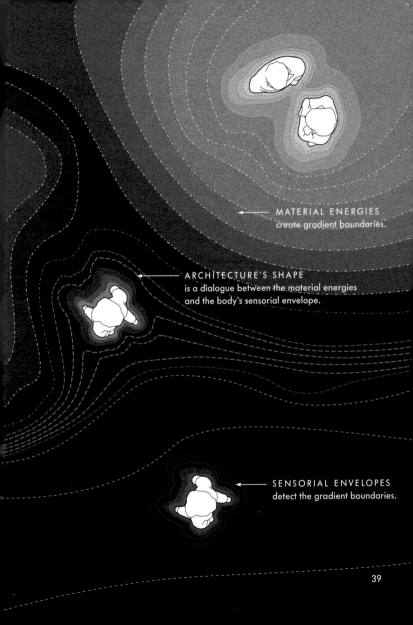

MATERIAL ENERGIES
create gradient boundaries.

ARCHITECTURE'S SHAPE
is a dialogue between the material energies
and the body's sensorial envelope.

SENSORIAL ENVELOPES
detect the gradient boundaries.

AMPLIFICATION

Architecture today, much as it did several thousand years ago, attempts to extend Earth's outer shell—the surface on which we stand—by adding other shells of our own making. Materials of stone, steel, concrete, and glass—refinements of the existing geologic layer—form artificial masses, or buildings, that produce new pockets of space. As these built forms rise from Earth's surface, they engage with the planet's atmosphere. In fact, it would be more useful to say that we "live not on the summit of a solid earth, but rather at the bottom of an ocean of air."[1] And so, as architecture continues to build up Earth's outermost shell by mimicking, embellishing, and enhancing the materials that constitute that layer, the question arises: Why hasn't architecture sought to pursue a similar approach with the materials comprising this "ocean" of air, our atmosphere, in order to further create new spaces?

Architects have not asked the various forms of energy that make up this ocean of air to do much more than reproduce and mimic an ideal climate, remaining passive when they actually have the potential to play a more active role. Much like gravity, energy behaves in particular ways that are impossible to overlook. Yet we rarely think of gravity as we do the outer environment, as merely an obstacle to be overcome. Instead, it is a design opportunity to subvert and play against, with cantilevers and slender structures. Surrounding forms of energy present similar opportunities, but when architects do look to the environment that exists beyond their architectural envelopes for inspiration, the focus seems more on viewing biological specimens as structural and geometric models while ignoring the energy systems that influence and act on those specimens. We seem more drawn to imitate the voluptuous shape and texture of the durian fruit of Southeast Asia or the lengthy spine patterns of the pincushion cactus of western North America than in simulating the differing environmental variables these specimens live within. In adopting these biological forms via analogy and imitation, we place more value on the geometries of the vegetation than on the atmospheric and chemical properties of the context that helped inform their creation in the first place.

Architects have never been modest in the scope and ambition of their projects, taking the opportunity to design everything from entire cities to the teaspoon used to stir your sugar in its matching cup. But it would seem that the profession has developed a rather large blind spot in terms of what it sees as malleable material for architects to engage. By making assumptions as to what might be beyond its purview, architects have refrained from engaging a fuller range of possible material variables. We are continuously enveloped by a wide range of energy systems touching both the exteriors and the interiors of our buildings, but we think these particles, waves, and frequencies are too faint or shaky or unwieldy to create the secure physical boundaries we associate with architecture. This has resulted in a cultivated set of blinders that characterizes architecture as an assembly of mediation devices (surfaces, walls, and inert masses) that separate individuals and activities placed on one side from the larger context beyond. These mediation devices temper both existing climates as well as man-made energy systems, including sounds from traffic and light pollution, that together create the *environmental contexts* architecture exists within. Such a mediating architecture is defined by its ability to decide what gets in (breezes, light) and what stays out (precipitation, cold winds). We place organizational demands and aesthetic meaning onto the surfaces, walls, and masses that mediate these energy variables, rather than seeing the energy systems themselves as available for manipulation as a building material of their own.

The starting point here is a rather naive and fundamental question: can we design the energy systems that course in and around us every day, and use them as a material that meets the needs associated with architecture (shaping activities, security, and lifestyle)? Can the variables that we would normally mediate instead be amplified to become architectural materials and, in turn, architecture itself? What many would incorrectly dismiss as simply "air" today—thought to be homogeneous, scaleless, and vacant due in part to the limits of our human sensory system to perceive otherwise—might tomorrow be so articulat-

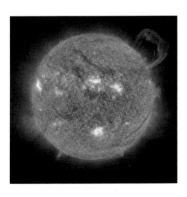

RADIATION
The particles and waves of the sun's radiation that interact with all matter on this planet have the potential to become a set of materials for building new forms of architectural space.

ed, strengthened, and layered as to become a material for building boundaries, defining individuals' movements, and generating architectural space. The environmental context that engulfs us all, the lowest level of that vast ocean of air above us, is more than sunlight, wind, and precipitation—elements for architecture to select, reject, or recreate in our interiors. It is also the *material energies* of electromagnetics, thermodynamics, acoustic waves, and chemical interactions, which we know surround us constantly, yet have refrained so far from using as architectural building blocks.

Mark Wigley's assertion that "all architecture is a form of radiation" throws these possibilities that architects might be overlooking into sharp relief.[2] Starting from his statement, one can imagine that architecture has a broader bandwidth to work within than we've previously assumed. One kind of radiation comes from the sun; through a combination of factors (including our sun's radiation spectrum, our planet's distance from it, and the filtering effects of Earth's atmosphere), the resulting sunlight that reaches our planet's surface is within a visible spectrum from violet to red.[3] Blue photons carry some of the strongest levels of energy, while red photons carry less energy but are more constant. Plants absorb the energy from sunlight to power photosynthesis, leaving the green wavelengths to bounce back and create the color that our eyes see. It's no coincidence that our eyes have adapted to perceive sunlight, the strongest spectrum of radiation to reach the Earth's surface; after all, this energy supports almost all life on the planet.

However, should any of the aforementioned variables have differed in any way—should Earth have swerved off course a few million years ago, several million miles to the "left" or a few hundred thousand miles to the "right"—the most energy-packed spectrum of the sun's radiation reaching Earth could very well have been deep violet or maybe something near infrared.[4] Either of these spectrums could have powered a very different type of photosynthesis, and our plant material would look altogether different, too. We could very well be touting a "red" revolution in environmental activism instead of a "green" one right now, with an architecture interested in identifying itself as environmentally sensitive assuming the mantras and slogans of "red architecture," like one imagines would exist on the Martian territories of H. G. Wells's *War of the Worlds*.[5] Rather than green, the color that plants reflect back to us could range from what the Pantone color chart refers to as "bland" to color #EE2C55, a dark red labeled "awesome." Who wouldn't enjoy an "awesome" architecture or environmental revolution over a green one? It is possible that on such an Earth, the chemical compositions of the atmosphere would include a different ratio of nitrogen and oxygen, sounds would travel at a different rate, temperatures would be different, and its inhabitants' sensory perceptions would have evolved to interact with all these new variables.

The point to be made here is that just as Earth's mass defines the force of gravity that our buildings and bodies must stand up against, Earth's distance from the sun dictates the spectrum of energy that informs life and how we differentiate between one microclimate or ecosystem and another. These are the rule sets we use—the laws we are tied to as they relate to behaviors. And even though Earth won't be changing its location in the solar system anytime soon, nor will the energy from the sun that reaches its surface shift outside of the visible spectrum, this doesn't preclude our manipulation of the material variables currently accessible. Much as in their interactions with gravity, architects can't alter such laws, but they can work with the full range of materials that are governed by them. Like the steel, stone, or glass we manipulate to defy gravity, the material variables associated with and tied to energy (the waves, particles, and chemical compositions of our atmospheres) can each be defined as a materiality once their properties and behaviors can be controlled enough to be shaped and maintained over time. Unlike the laws that govern their behavior, these energies are malleable, not static and unwavering, and can be augmented, mutated, and designed as materials to shape our environments and architecture.

ENVIRONMENTAL DESIGN

Geometry has long been architecture's way of articulating material control, and the profession's ability to manipulate geometries and surfaces has evolved in that time. Similarly, the means for understanding and manipulating our chemical and gaseous context have become increasingly sophisticated as well. The discovery and manipulation of these energies had an especially rich lineage between the seventeenth and eighteenth centuries, particularly when seen against the backdrop of what the arts and architecture were also investigating at the time. As architects experimented with fluid, highly expressive surfaces, projecting new cultural and organizational ambitions onto stone, masonry, and glass, scientific inquiry regarding the makeup of the atmospheric volumes that moved in and around these forms was simultaneously under way. The High Baroque is exemplified by

"SOLID" BUILDING
BLOCKS
Top left: Transparency, Con-
stance Perkins House by Richard
Neutra (1955). Top right:
Malleability of forms with
reinforced concrete, TWA
Terminal by Eero Saarinen
(1962). Bottom: Increased
spans through the use of steel,
Art Center College of Design
by Craig Ellwood (1976).

Amplification

Francesco Borromini's mid-seventeenth century San Carlo alle Quattro Fontane, which demonstrated an ability to deliver a sense of plasticity through geometry, evident in its façade, as well as on the interior surface of the dome and in its planimetric organization of space. At around roughly the same time, Johann Baptista van Helmont, a Flemish chemist sometimes referred to as the founder of pneumatic chemistry,[6] used the word "gas" for the first time to define specific properties within atmospheric air that represented a state of matter other than solid or liquid. Even as Gian Lorenzo Bernini, in his *Ecstasy of St. Teresa*, was producing in stone the lightness of clouds and a billowing of robes that obtain a near weightlessness, Pierre Petit was confirming Blaise Pascal's theory that atmosphere has weight by carrying a barometer to the top of a mountain to show that atmospheric pressure decreases with height.[7] And nearly seventy years before cast-iron and glass-frame public exhibition structures would emerge in nineteenth-century England and France to enclose exotic climates and expansive interiors of vegetation, Carl Scheele, a pharmaceutical chemist, became one of the first to synthesize oxygen in his laboratory.[8]

Even prior to these scientific experiments and discoveries, the impact of "vapors" on those encountering them was well known. Volatile gases buried in the soils of swamps, bogs, mines, or quarries—these pockets of putrid air where vegetation, water, and fish carcasses had decayed often reemerged when land was drained and later plowed—were widely feared long before science could entirely understand them, because their release could strike an individual dead.[9] But to see the scientific discoveries of the makeup and properties of gases like these coinciding with

PLASTICITY,
LIGHTNESS, AND
ARTIFICIAL CLIMATES
Top left: San Carlo alle
Quattro Fontane (1638–1641),
interior by Francesco
Borromini. Top right: *Ecstasy
of Saint Teresa* (1647–1652)
by Gian Lorenzo Bernini.
Bottom: Palm House in the
Royal Botanical Gardens
(1844–1848), Kew / Surrey,
England, by Decimus Burton
and Richard Turner.

architectural tendencies that seem to be demanding similar performative characteristics from solid materials like stone (from the lightness and buoyancy exemplified in Bernini's sculptures, to the malleability traced from the exterior to the interior of Baroque churches, to the artificial climates trapped within expansive iron and glass shells) is intriguing. Was the virtuosity of the architects and artists of the era tied to their ability to depict such qualities in inert materials like stone and iron where others before them could not? Or is it that they sought them out in the first place, setting the stage for a moment when scientific understanding would allow atmospheric qualities to eventually perform architecturally themselves?

As an understanding of the chemical makeup of our atmospheric surroundings progressed during the next century, it made its most striking and public debut in the development of military weaponry during the First World War, when weapons designers began engaging the very environment the human body moves through as never before. Peter Sloterdijk has stated that the real "discovery" of the environment took place as gas warfare was waged in the trenches of World War I; instead of targeting the body of the enemy through physical projectiles (bullets, rockets, missiles), warring nations instead made the environment itself impossible for the enemy to exist in.[10] This "targeting" of enemy soldiers' environmental context with poison gas was utilized on such a mass scale during the second battle of Ypres on April 22, 1915,[11] that it is believed that nearly a third of the casualties were related to the deployment of chlorine gas.

To overcome the deadly chemical alteration to the air that our respiratory and vital organs rely on, scientists developed a means of defense—specifically, masks that protected the eyes, mouth, and nose. These enclosures surrounding the face mediated between the body and the gas around it, producing a hermetically sealed cavity that could filter and guard against the toxic context that existed on the other side of that rubberized-canvas and glass boundary. The environmental context was hostile, so the mask produced an independent context, forming a "bubble" that enclosed the body in order to protect it and allow it to move about unaffected by what was outside.

The focus here goes beyond the scientific discoveries that produced the lethal gas itself. Rather, the emphasis is on the gas's chemical distortion of the environment that the body moves through and how the human senses can thus be targeted in a manipulated environmental context. In the fields where it was released, the gas formed geographically specific boundaries between areas of different chemical concentrations; these boundaries were less hard lines than gradient edges that marked a varying degree of enclosure, with soldiers either near the periphery of the gas or deep inside it where its effects were most strongly felt. These pockets and fronts of intensity demarcated and subdivided the battleground, influenced the movement and strategic deployment of soldiers, and at times pulled their bodies into its interior when the winds unexpectedly shifted. Carried by the winds, the particles would eventually dissipate, but for a period of time, physical territories were formed in which the body could locate itself as being inside the gas, on its periphery, or outside the gas.

So, the early twentieth century showed that we could not only chemically manipulate the environment our bodies move in, but also provide individual bubbles for our bodies to move through that manipulated context unharmed. Given a choice between these two extremely different directions in material manipulation, it's clear that architecture has continued in the direction of the filtering mask. In doing so, the discipline reinforced its ongoing commitment to architecture's mediating context, choosing not to engage the possibility of explicitly designing the chemical and energy systems already coursing (like poison gas) through a site.

By the time the gas mask was put into use in military battles, over a half century of experimentation had already occurred in building technology seeking a similar type of control. In this case, it was control over the moisture and air quality in factories needed to help stabilize and increase production levels. Willis Carrier coined the term "air-conditioning" in 1914, giving a name that we use still to this day to the augmentation of the air within the interiors of buildings. It was common practice in factories prior to this work, whether they refined cotton or chocolate, to stop production if the existing humidity and temperature began affecting the product or the machinery producing it. Much like the gas mask that separated a soldier's respiratory system and eyes from a poisoned context, a filtration system was developed for factories that could manage these variables and prevent work stoppages and losses of quality control. To maintain the artificial climates thus produced, architects sealed the perimeters of buildings to maximize this control and minimize any potential interference by exterior variables. This also prevented the escape of the cooled and dehumidified air that had taken so much effort to create in the first place. Although the political, moral, and economic considerations behind these two examples are widely different, their shared logic makes both of them representative of technological forays into environmental mediation.

As architects and engineers followed the directives of environmental separation and control, building envelopes and mechanical systems became the hallmarks of the profession. Innovation was understood to take place in envelope technology (rain screens, waterproof membranes, glazing, insulation) and in the systems for producing climatic control, rather than in the engineering and architectural control of the material variables that existed on the other side of the surface envelope. The gas mask that protected the eyes and nose from a poisoned environment became an appropriate analogy for homes and public buildings that would seal themselves off so as to heat and cool

GAS WARFARE AND THE MEDIATING MASK
Gas warfare first appeared during the second battle of Ypres on April 22, 1915, with the deployment of chlorine gas.

their interiors and filter the variables—sun, winds, and odor—of the outside world.

MEDIATION TOOK CONTROL

Mediation is a long-running trajectory in the architectural profession, and although it certainly intensifies with the advent of air-conditioning, it did not originate in the early twentieth century. Mediation is an act that by its nature selects and rejects variables within the environmental context, picking and choosing which qualities can be used for the benefit of the activities occurring on the other side of the mediating surface and which need to be rejected and protected against. Manifestations include not only the building envelope but also the use of vegetation on the exteriors of buildings, as in the case of tree canopies in gardens that create shade. Architecture in which an "interior" space directly opens to the context beyond it only exists when that exterior climate or context is neutral enough to accommodate such an attempt. Some of the most well-known examples of this are the Case Study Houses of Southern California, designed during the mid-twentieth century with sliding-glass exterior walls and floor materials that extend from the interior to the exterior so as to provide seamless transitions between the two states. But even in the temperate weather of Southern California, closed glass doors provided a thermal boundary, and eaves extended beyond the rooflines to provide shade and protection from rain. The use of steel and glass only saw to it that the materials that provided mediation were less visible, allowing for a transparency that further reinforced the impression of seamlessness from one side of the mediating envelope to the other. The surfaces of a building, whether made of brick, concrete, glass, mesh, or any form of perforated surface material including apertures, form the outlines of an array of building typologies set to mediate the environmental context and define the spaces for activities inside.

Such surfaces, there to temper the climatic variables that affect our bodies and activities, fall within what Reyner Banham has categorized as three main areas of performance: conservative, selective, and generative.[12] The conservative performance requires a wall and its materials to provide a thermal lag that limits heat from entering during the day yet radiates absorbed heat at night to warm the interior. Think of adobe structures or a concrete parking garage in Las Vegas at two in the morning that is warmer inside than the surrounding sidewalks as the concrete slowly releases the heat collected from absorbing the sun's energy all day. The selective performance derives from adapting exterior walls, roofs, and floors to filter existing breezes and provide shade from the sun, all in an attempt to mediate existing conditions within the interior or beyond that surface. Examples of selective surfaces include porches, brise soleil, and canopies of building overhangs or trees. And thirdly, the generative performance relies on the sealing and closing of these surfaces to permit artificial heating and cooling systems to mechanically provide the desired level of comfort on the interior.[13] Each of these performances prioritizes the physical, built surface, with the possible exception of the generative, where mechanical equipment plays a primary role, though even in this case the surface is the line of demarcation for what stays in and what gets out as it seals the building off from its surroundings.

Further, given advancements in curtain wall construction that mean the outer surfaces no longer provide the structural support of the building, today many such surfaces are solely mediation devices for defining interior space. Contemporary design culture in particular, which focuses on form-finding strategies and scripting logics for designing complex surfaces, and which believes that innovation exists only within geometry, has resulted in reinforcing an architecture defined by mediation. The quest for more complex walls has been taken up with such maniacal attention that discussions of the energy found between and around these walls have been largely avoided. This trajectory of mediation hasn't wavered, even as techniques for visualizing a wider array of these energy systems have become available thanks to software simulation; as of now, little is asked from these energies and their software simulations beyond help in reproducing and imitating "ideal" climates to supply a rather subjective level of comfort to our bodies.

The focus, then, is on interior climatic homogeneity. So it is not surprising that the idea of context is generally understood within architecture practice as something to respond to, whether that means tying a project back to infrastructural systems (e.g., roads), or tapping an existing resource, or relating the project to a building near its site, or mediating the environmental conditions associated with solar orientation, optimal views, or existing climate. As in the example of gas warfare, however, we can and do intentionally influence our environmental context; we simply don't do it under the guise of architectural (spatial and organizational) design. Instead, the ways that architecture already affects our environmental context every day is viewed as a by-product condition, often unintentional, and certainly not in any way controlled for architecture's benefit. We only need to look to the heat island effect in cities like Atlanta and Houston, created by large expanses of materials with low albedo levels (like asphalt) that absorb energy from the sun, or the microclimates that form outside buildings as a result of exhausted excess heat from mechanical systems, computers, and human bodies, to see that we actually do shape these local climates. Even the most passive building exceeds its formal constructs once you consider the shadows cast from its volume, the winds it produces or blocks, and the solar radiation reflected from its glass surfaces. But these are accidental conditions, fallout of the built environment, with no real intention to dictate organizational and spatial strategies.

Architects have argued that architecture requires walls and surfaces in order to provide for the needs of the human body and its activities. Questioning this assumption is not only to open a discussion of what types of materials can construct architecture, but also to ask what opportunities and implications might arise for the very activities and social interactions that are propelled and controlled by this change in material boundaries, including our bodies' relationships to these environmental materials. Mediation of environmental energies controls their relationship to the body, or a desired activity beyond, but it does not alter the energies' makeup. If, however, those environmental energies could be amplified and strengthened, they themselves could become the materials used to build architecture. Being able to amplify energy to control a spatial boundary or provide a resource so an activity can occur makes that type of energy a material, one that the architect can design with. Amplification is the act of working the various forms of energy available into materials that can build architecture.

AMPLIFICATION

Some of the most interesting and unexpected illustrations of the idea of amplifying the environmental context to form architecture can be found in the buildings of the 2008 Summer Olympics in Beijing. At first, the colossal collection of stadiums produced for the event seemed to be a showcase for façade design and curtain wall construction more than anything else. As the Games approached, however, discussion turned to the air quality within the venues (and the notoriously polluted city overall) and the potential impact this would have on the performance of the athletes. (In fact, the city strictly prevented the use of cars and vehicles for several days leading up to the Games in order to reduce particulates in the air.)

So many aspects of Olympic sports are meticulously monitored and controlled, from the chemical supplements that athletes consume to the equipment they use (whether swimsuits or bikes). Yet the environmental parameters that athletes' bodies move through are often left to be determined by the existing conditions of a specified calendar day and geographic location. Issues of environmental context are addressed only in the broadest sense when choosing where to locate the Olympics for a particular year (and then primarily in hoping for good weather). On the other hand, knowledge that the environmental context plays a role in affecting competitive sports is widespread: runners, for instance, know that their performance is tied to the air's oxygen content, making it common practice to train in the days leading up to a race at higher elevations, where oxygen levels are lower, hence increasing their endurance when they return to lower elevations with higher concentrations of oxygen.

Competitive swimming is the event where the relationship between the context and the body that moves through it is most clearly foregrounded. As always, there were discussions at the 2008 Olympics regarding the potential to gain unfair advantage from the technologies and gear used by the athletes. In the case of swimming, the issue was the use of one-piece swimsuits that covered the body from the ankle to the neck. Some swimmers even wore more than one suit so as to create buoyancy from the air pockets that formed between the two layers. Evidence suggests that these concerns were valid: in 2008 alone, seventy swimming world records were broken, sixty-six records were broken in the Olympic games, and there were races in which the first five finishers were ahead of the existing Olympic record.[14] By 2010, regulations had been passed stating that "men swimsuits [sic] shall not extend above the navel or below the knee" in an attempt to bring an element of fair play back to the sport.[15]

Regardless of the suits swimmers wear, the actual medium that each moves through is equal to all, giving no one competitor an unfair advantage. Improving upon this neutral medium—in other words, introducing changes that provide equal benefit to all swimmers—is referred to in swimming as creating "faster pools." A "faster pool" results from deploying a series of techniques in the design of a pool to lessen resistance for swimmers as they move through the water, leading to faster times. The depth of the pool, the extra swimming lanes and overflow gutters on the sides of the pool, and the line ropes that separate the swim lanes (known as wave eaters) are design elements that can be manipulated to reduce the interference and turbulence given off by the swimmers, making the pool faster for all.

Faster pools represent an enhancement of context that allows the sport to evolve, generating new excitement for viewers (and sponsors) by extending the limits of what has been previously possible—take the attention garnered by swimmer Michael Phelps in both 2008 and 2012, for example. Knowing that controversy arises when individuals are suspected of pursuing unfair advantages through the gear they have access to and/or by chemically enhancing their bodies, Olympic officials prefer to look toward the playing fields that the sports take place on to meet these pressures for advancement.

However, one of the questions raised during the 2008 Games by former Olympic medalist and swimming commentator Rowdy Gaines was whether this particular pool—The Beijing National Aquatic Center—had reached the apex of pool design through these techniques, which were based, as all pool designs are, in shaping the geometries that hold the pool water.[16] Gaines suggested that if pools are going to get faster, if records are going to continually be broken, the focus of pool design might move beyond molding the surfaces that mediate the turbulence and currents within the water by dissipation or absorption to augmenting the water itself that fills the shape![17] He proposed, in other words, a focus on the design of the water. The architectural opportunity no longer is in the shell that caps the space (that is, the swimming pool edges), but in the physical context through which the athletes move. A new frontier in swimming performance might exist in the evaluation of the chemical make-up of the water itself, in the salinity, buoyancy, and chemical components of the water and its feedback relationship to the athlete's movements. The environmental context the athletes move through thus becomes a focus of design attention, just like

ARCHITECTURE THROUGH AMPLIFICATION
Top: Beijing National Aquatics Center (2008) by PTW Architects, CSCEC, CCDI, and Arup. Under construction with an empty pool; the geometries of construction hold the activities inside. Bottom: Manipulating the properties of water that the bodies move through is the next medium for design.

the structures that shape the pool's outer forms or the equipment that the athletes currently use in competition. Looking to strengthen the chemical composition of the water to accommodate the needs of open athletic competition is a promising option and an immense incentive that can't help but spark the imagination of the architect.

Pool water now is treated much as architecture treats its interiors: as something to merely be tempered and kept sanitary. Setting the temperature of Olympic pool water at 77–82 degrees Fahrenheit, and using filtration and chlorine to prevent algae infections and keep the water clean, is not much different from maintaining a building's internal air temperature at 68–72 degrees Fahrenheit with 45 percent relative humidity and filtering out undesirable air particles. The temperature control and cleaning that occur now in pool water represent an elimination (or mediation) of variables, not a creation of new ones. Much like our climatic interior controls, these interventions are specified to create a baseline that has been formulated from ideas of an existing ideal condition—in this case, a clean, temperate, and waveless open body of water. But unlike the surface of running tracks or the artificial turf of soccer and football fields, pool water is something that the body moves *through*. Pool water is a step beyond. It deals with more than engineering a product that increases the performance of the human body or relocating an event from one oxygen-specific altitude to another. Changing the properties of the space through which athletes move is designing their environmental context. To do this, architects must engage the materialities associated with the environmental context, amplifying and controlling them with the same fervor they have applied to the construction of the surfaces used to mediate against that same environmental context for so many millennia.

We can all recognize one of the most elemental versions of such an amplification: the results of the heat released from a city's infrastructure systems or a building's mechanical system running under an outdoor expanse during the winter months. As exhaust grates release excess energy onto grassy patches outside, the micro-local temperature builds up with the expended heat, warming the soil and surrounding air. Where snow and ice cover the surrounding region, plants have gone dormant, but this little swatch of area shows contrasting signs of growing grass, along with melted snow and the gathering of people to stay warm. This anomalous pocket defines a local geography within a broader context. Such contrasting microclimates exist nearly

THIS IS NOT WEATHER CONTROL
Unlike the image of a snowstorm in a forest on a summer's day, the attempt here is not to condition exterior spaces as we currently do our interiors, but to produce architectural shapes and spaces free from comparisons to existing weather or ecological systems. Image: *Midsummer Snow Storm* by Peter Liversidge (2009).

everywhere, from the geothermal pools of Iceland to the oases formed by underground rivers and aquifers in deserts from the Sahara to Peru. Energy dumps at the exteriors of buildings are not much different from these natural examples, though the dumps are singular and simplistic in their deployment since they are essentially a defect condition, unplanned by anyone. They rarely have intricacies with nested subsets; instead, they act under binary "on" and "off" conditions. But they do point us in the direction of how a primitive example might be intensified and layered with multiple material energies and specified design intentions, providing more than a pocket of heat on a cold day. These accidental hiccups on grassy patches outside buildings are only a glimmer of the diverse constructs and worlds to be devised.

Architecture formed through amplification engages the existing energy systems within our surrounding environment, intensifying and fortifying them to become architectural materials. In doing so, those new material energies absorb the spatial and organizational responsibilities that currently reside in architectural surfaces. The spaces thus created are compositions of materials already around us that are charged with chemical and electrical properties. The intensification of the environmental context that the body moves through creates a layered makeup of particulates working together in parallel, overlapping with and integrated into one another. Like a body of water with currents, an amplified surrounding environment would be defined by thermoclines that would often be sudden and striking in their contrasts with one another and their surroundings, producing new edges and boundaries in space. As currents of energies course through sites at varying frequencies and intensities, each would engage the sensory perceptions of the body differently.

Amplification of the existing energies of our surrounding context shouldn't be confused with reconstructing a climatic ideal. It is more than simply "conditioning" exterior spaces or producing recognizable climates. History can point us to numerous architectural "weather control" strategies, but what is sought here isn't the culling of recognizable climates to achieve preconceived specifications associated with existing lifestyles, as in climate-controlled interiors. Instead, amplification allows architecture to explore new territories of design, aesthetic proclivities, and social interaction. When a wall is no longer the standard organizational device, it takes very little imagination to see that new organizational strategies might also be put into play, even when they are not always immediately apparent.

A false duality persists behind our actions as they pertain to our surroundings that limits us either to poisoning the environment or to conserving it—a belief that if you are not involved in reducing energy consumption or in remediating the environment around you in some fashion, you are complicit in its destruction. What this perspective ignores is the constant immediacy of our environment, the fact that we are always interacting with our surroundings in subtle ways that are also rife with potential for manipulation. The context that our bodies move through daily is a material ready for our design engagement. As humans, we have never lived in an elevated position somehow disengaged from our environmental context. Producing an architecture through the amplification of the energy systems already surrounding us is more than displacing activities and events associated with our interiors (sheltered behind mediating surfaces) to the "outside." It's also a reconfiguration of the physical boundaries that organize these activities, a shift that will have fundamental repercussions on the very definitions of the activities we design for and the environments within which our architecture exists.

1 "Torricelli a Michelangelo Ricci in Roma, Firenze, 11 Giugno 1644," in *Opere dei Discepoli di Galileo, Carteggio 1642-1648*, eds. P. Galluzzi e M. Torrini, vol. 1 (Florence: Giunti-Barbera, 1975), 122, 123. This quote is often associated with the sixth-century BC writer Thales of Miletus, but it seems more likely to have come from Torricelli in a letter to Michelangelo Ricci. Thanks to Jackie Murray for this help.

2 Mark Wigley, "The Architecture of the Leap," in *Yves Klein: Air Architecture*, eds. Peter Noever and Francois Perrin (Los Angeles: MAK Center for Art and Architecture, 2004), 113.

3 Nancy Y. Kiang, "The Color of Plants on Other Worlds," *Scientific American* (April 2008), 50. Kiang discusses how distance correlates to the strength of radiation as it travels from the sun. If plants were to exist on other planets, they would likely require different forms of photosynthesis and energy frequencies from one planet to another.

4 Ibid., 55.

5 Ibid., 50.

6 Eric John Holmyard, *Makers of Chemistry* (Oxford: Oxford University Press, 1931), 121.

7 "Discovering Air," *NOVA Online*, Public Broadcasting Service, http://www.pbs.org/wgbh/nova/everest/earth/air.html (accessed 14 October 2012).

8 See Thomas S. Kuhn, *The Structure of Scientific Revolutions*, 3rd ed. (Chicago: University of Chicago Press: 1996), 52–55, for a discussion of the multiple people working on this discovery separately over several years. This has made it difficult to specify one individual for the discovery. Kuhn describes in these pages the difficulty of pinpointing specific dates and people responsible for a given scientific discovery due to the scientific process.

9 Alain Corbin, "The Extremes of Olfactory Vigilance," in *The Foul and the Fragrant: Odor and the French Social Imagination* (Cambridge, MA: Harvard University Press, 1988), 34.

10 Peter Sloterdijk, *Terror from the Air*, trans. Amy Patton and Steve Corcoran (Los Angeles: Semiotext(e), 2009), 18, 14.

11 Ibid., 29.

12 Reyner Banham, *The Architecture of the Well-Tempered Environment* (Chicago: University of Chicago Press, 1969), 23. Banham discusses three recognized techniques for dealing with existing climatic conditions: "Conservative," "Selective," and "Generative."

13 This discussion is well covered by Gail Cooper's *Air-Conditioning America* (Baltimore: Johns Hopkins University Press, 1998), as well as in writing by Michelle Addington, and therefore won't be covered in further detail here.

14 "FINA Requirements for Swimwear Approval," Federation Internationale de Natation, http://www.fina.org/H2O/docs/rules/SWIMWEAR_APPROVAL_from_01012010 (accessed 14 October 2012).

15 Ibid.

16 Howard Berkes, "China's Olympic Swimming Pool: Redefining Fast," *Weekend Edition Sunday*, National Public Radio, 10 August 2008, http://www.npr.org/templates/story/story.php?storyId=93478073 (accessed 14 October 2012).

17 Ibid.

The mounded roof shapes maintain artificial microclimates fed by energy dumps, creating climatically elastic spaces for social and communal activities as a resource for both the museum and the city of Gdansk.

Excess energy from the building's mechanical systems, parking structures located directly under the roof, and the combined body heat of several thousand visitors a day is collected and reused on the roof during winter months.

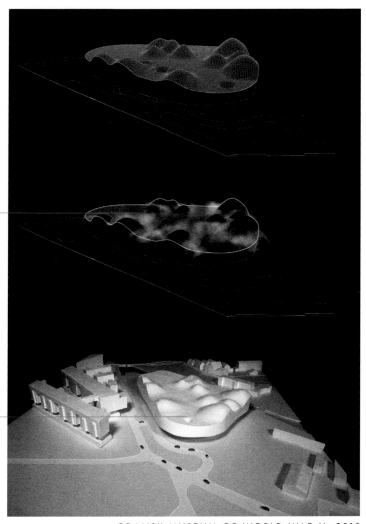

GDANSK MUSEUM OF WORLD WAR II, 2010
Renderings/Model
Sean Lally WEATHERS

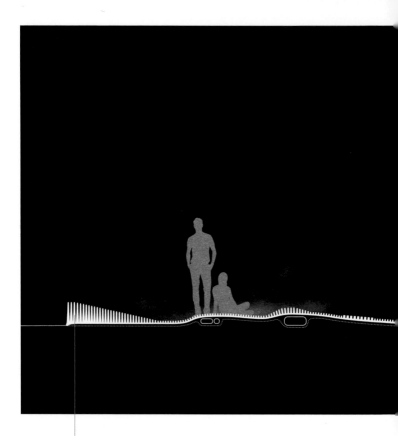

Shagg continues where Astroturf left off, using
a groundcover system to shape distinct exterior spaces
that people can engage and use regardless of existing
environmental forces like weather or noise from traffic.

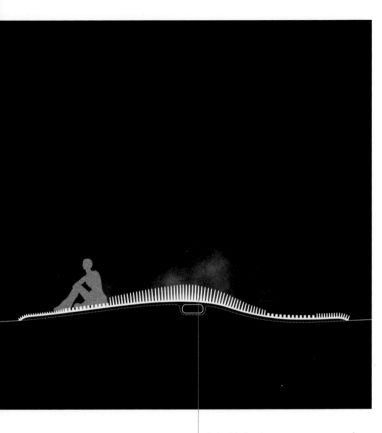

Embedded in the carpet are sources of
light, heat, and noise cancellation
techniques, which work in combination to
define unique spatial conditions.

SHAGG, 2009–2010
Section
Sean Lally WEATHERS

AMPLIFICATION, 2006–2007
Sean Lally WEATHERS

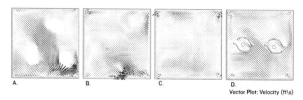

A.   B.   C.   D.
Vector Plot: Velocity (ft\s)

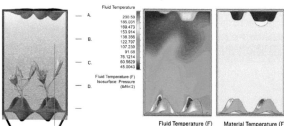

Fluid Temperature

— A.

— B.

— C.

— D.

—

200.59
185.031
169.473
153.914
138.356
122.797
107.239
91.68
76.1214
60.5629
45.0043

Fluid Temperature (F)
Isosurface: Pressure
(lbf/in^2)

Fluid Temperature (F)   Material Temperature (F)

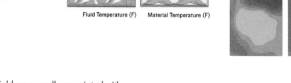

Variables generally associated with
a garden, including light, temperature,
scent, and air velocity, are uniquely
controlled in each of the six units in an
attempt to produce distinct microclimates
in and around those shapes.

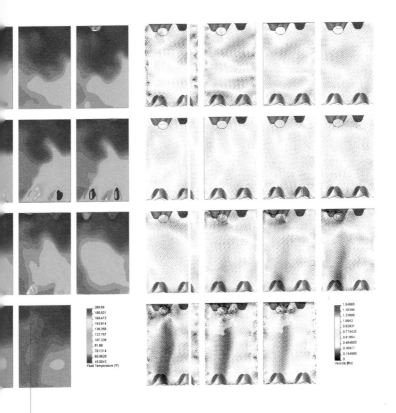

Simulations in COSMOS (a computational
fluid dynamic modeling software) permit
a visualization of material energies, including
thermal transfers and changes in air velocity.

AMPLIFICATION, 2006–2007
Simulations
Sean Lally WEATHERS

Existing climate and seasonal variability (artificial or otherwise) is just as important a consideration for urban organization as the structures built to house specific programs. Local climatic manipulations are made possible by harnessing the available energy as a form of infrastructure.

These gradient parks shift in size and intensity with seasonal changes, often spilling out and connecting with each other in milder seasons while shrinking and acting as disparate entities in the more extreme winter months.

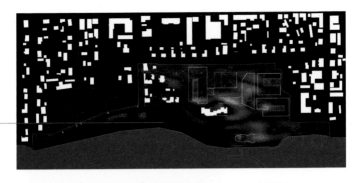

TAMULA LAKESIDE, 2008
Site Plan
Sean Lally WEATHERS

The glass pyramidal shapes span the voids in each building's mass. By capping the voids, they trap energy from the sun and building systems, transferring it through the voids and onto the landscape below.

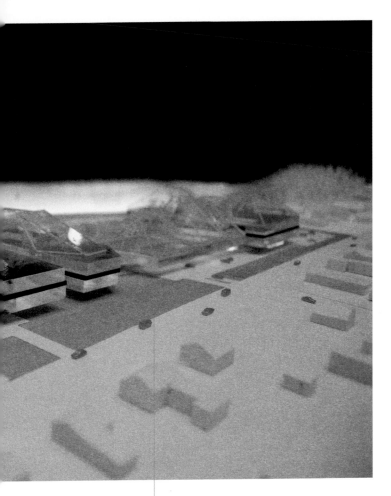

To visually connect the city of Võru to the lakefront, the buildings have been lifted off the ground. The landscape opened up in this way is reconnected and organized by the six energy pockets under the pyramids.

TAMULA LAKESIDE, 2008
Model
Sean Lally WEATHERS

An enlarged and exaggerated double-skin curtain wall enables energy to be trapped and then deployed outward to engage the surrounding site. Smaller seating systems located on the ground plane also serve to distribute the energies locally.

This trapped energy defines flexible spatial zones for the entrance, restaurant, and meeting centers that are capable of changing in scale and intensity based on their interplay with the existing climate and time of year in Stockholm.

ASPLUND LIBRARY ADDITION, 2006
Model
Sean Lally WEATHERS

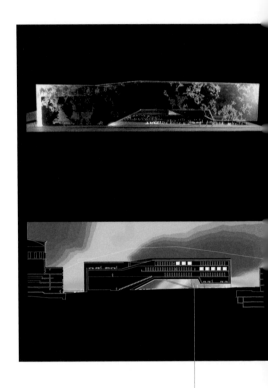

The interior black masses act as a depository for
programs that require stricter environmental control,
including book storage and administrative offices.
These masses maximize surface area to produce the
enlarged double-skin curtain wall.

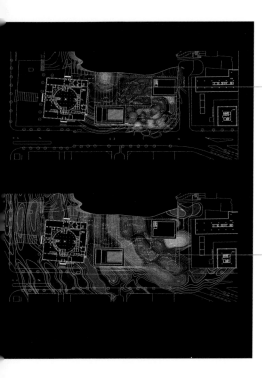

The gradient architectural spaces created by the trapped energy are expected to fluctuate in size because of a continuous feedback relationship between the existing climate and these spaces, which exchange energy, informing their spatial and aesthetic characteristics.

The library addition operates beyond the envelope of the building—and at times beyond the boundary of the site—as it engages and rewrites the surrounding climatic and environmental properties.

ASPLUND LIBRARY ADDITION, 2006
Model / Section / Site Plans
Sean Lally WEATHERS

Six "climatic lungs" set within the building's mass visually connect the design schools and administration above to a year-round public park below. This ceiling plan acts as the building's most public façade.

The park, in turn, sits on top of art galleries, a black box theater, and conference rooms, as well as mechanical systems and an entire floor of college wood and metal workshops. These programs are sunk half a floor level, making the park easily accessible from the street. All excess energy from these programs is delivered into the soil and vegetation of the park located underneath the "lungs."

ESTONIAN ACADEMY OF ARTS, 2008
Model
Sean Lally WEATHERS

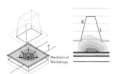 

Point sources allow climate control.

Upper levels utilize climate zones below. Lighting from below illuminates studio spaces above.

Variations in climate control create distinct zones.

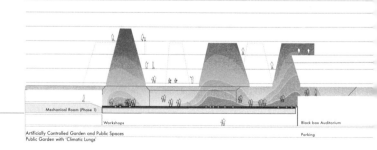

Mechanical Room (Phase 1)

Workshops

Black box Auditorium

Artificially Controlled Garden and Public Spaces

Parking

Public Garden with 'Climatic Lungs'

The school's public spaces are located on top of the building's primary mechanical systems and workshops, which are sunk half a story off the street; these park spaces collect and amplify the building's captured energy to produce lush artificial gardens.

The "climatic lungs" move up the building through three levels of studios, gathering the excess energy that is then delivered into the park. As heat rises toward the upper floors, it pools internally, making it possible for students to enter these spaces off their studios and benefit from the artificial microclimates created there.

ESTONIAN ACADEMY OF ARTS, 2008
Model
Sean Lally WEATHERS

MATERIAL ENERGIES

Material energies are intensified versions of the energies already around us (electromagnetic, thermodynamic, acoustic, and chemical); in the hands of architects, they create physical boundaries and edges that are used to define space, facilitate activities, organize hierarchies, provide security, and produce architectural shape. They are amplifications of the stimuli present in the environment that the human body detects and interacts with. Material energies inform the body's behavior in three distinct ways. *Physical* energies act on the body in ways that can't be avoided. This includes existing conditions that we assume remain relatively constant—gravity, for example—or conditions that can be tuned and targeted geographically to apply controlling force, such as using sound waves at a frequency that can be felt or using an electrically charged field to restrict access and movement. *Informational* energies do not restrict movement or access, but instead provide decision-making cues. This includes street lighting on a dark corner, which, because its spectrum of light is tuned to the human eye, can provide information about safety and where others might be gathered. Individuals can choose to move inside the light or pass through it. *Trophic* energies affect the metabolism of the body. One example is the use of light therapy to alleviate the seasonal affective disorder and associated depression caused by the reduced levels of light in winter months, a common use of light as a trophic stimulus.

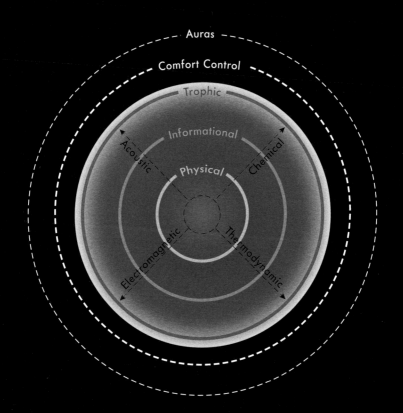

THE GRADIENT BOUNDARY

Material energies are defined by waves and particles, producing boundary edges that behave more like a gradient of intensities and fallouts, and less like the lines, points, or surfaces that the architectural profession is most familiar with. The behavior of material energies therefore can't be abstracted through the units of measurements and visualization tools most commonly taught in and associated with the profession of architecture. Dichotomies of solid versus void or black poché marks against a white page lose their significance when physical boundaries are instead understood in terms of intensities and rates of change. As our definition of an architectural boundary changes, so will the resultant spatial typologies that emerge over time. Designing with material energies is more than switching one material for another in the construction of architecture; it is realizing that the shift to a gradient boundary will have fundamental implications for how we represent and organize space.

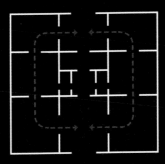

Necklace Circulation

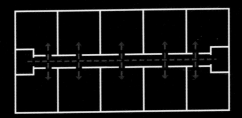

Corridors and Destinations

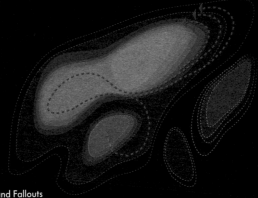

Intensities and Fallouts

ENVIRONMENTAL PUSHERS

Architecture inadvertently manipulates the environmental context we inhabit every day through the by-products of its very presence: building shadows, the release of excess energy from mechanical and shared city infrastructure systems, the creation of urban heat islands, and reflections from building façades. What architecture at present doesn't do is work with these manipulations as a design opportunity; instead, they are viewed only as unintentional remnants of current building and urban construction methodologies. In fact, these environmental alterations are resources of energy that can be controlled and adapted by the architect. Unlike solar or wind power, which harnesses energy, *environmental pushers* are by-product energy productions that can be put in the service of design. They are conditions either actively occurring within the urban infrastructure (venting, heat island effects) or assumed to occur in a proposed project (energy fallouts and dumps from mechanical systems, excess heat from computer use, body heat from large numbers of visitors). We currently manipulate local microclimates in our environments—it's just that we do it unintentionally.

Shadows

Reflections

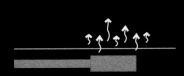

Infrastructure

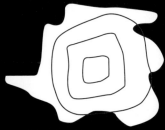

Urban Heat Islands

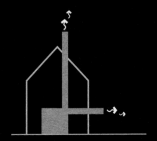

Energy Dumps

MATERIAL
ENERGIES

Over the last century and a half, architecture's relationship to its surrounding climate has advanced rather substantially, most notably in its ability to use mechanical systems to produce artificial climates inside sealed walls independently of outside factors (no existing breezes necessary). We've seen a progression from walls that simply temper local climate contexts to a collusion of wall construction technology and mechanical systems that ensures any interior climate is possible, regardless of what's happening outside. Coupled with advancements in visualization techniques, including software simulations of climatic energy behaviors, architects can now visualize and quantify not only temperature, but also humidity levels, airflow, light levels, and even the specified percentage of a desired air particulate to keep "clean rooms" clean. Looking to this trajectory, which has taken place over a rather short span of architectural history, one might ask: what is the next step. Will these mechanically devised climates of the interior subsume the very walls that hold them in? With such an action, the energies that are trapped inside hermetically sealed interiors will do more than duplicate "a good day outside" and will instead mature enough to absorb the architectural loads currently held by the surfaces and geometries closing in. When this occurs, those energies will become a set of building materials known as *material energies*.

Material energies are the stimuli and information within our surrounding context that the human body can perceive. More specifically, material energies produce the boundaries and edges that define space. This includes the full electromagnetic spectrum; the thermal properties of conduction, convection, and radiation; the acoustics associated with sound waves, both heard and felt; and the chemical compositions of the air we move through. For these forms of energy to be of use to architects, not only must they be quantifiable and controlled, but they must also be able to hold, in some manner, the spatial boundaries required of architecture and expected of the building materials they replace. This includes informing human behavior (directing movement and defining spatial hierarchies) as well as producing and maintaining the environmental variables that a specified activity requires. Material energies give the architect access to new types of boundary edges to work with in order to shape spaces.

The materials of interest here are familiar to all of us in a nascent state as either *auras* (lighting effects, atmospheric qualities, moods) or *comfort control* (air-conditioning, dehumidification, other forms of climate control). These materials until now have been relegated to conditioning predefined interiors or to acting as special effects in creating moods and theatrical atmospheres. In either case, the surface has been doing the heavy lifting, and the materials in question have simply played supporting roles. Yet the design profession might easily reconceive these auras or comfort controls so that they also take on a level of responsibility associated with defining physical boundaries (an inherent trait of architecture) and thus become material energies, building blocks that construct architectural space. "Responsibility" in this discussion shouldn't be confused with any moral or social imperative generally associated with energy conservation or preservation. Instead, the responsibility discussed here consists of taking on the tasks generally assigned to the surfaces and walls that provide the support enabling activities and events on a site to occur. This includes producing the physical boundaries of architecture, separating activities from each other, facilitating movement and circulation, and providing security and protection against unwanted external variables.

When architects design, they specify the properties of the physical boundaries that organize movements within a building or project and define the locations of events and actions; each of us is continuously aware of these boundaries and what they deny or allow us access to. Are there walls between you and where another activity is located? Are they transparent, opaque, or translucent? Are there doorways to where you want to go, or do you first need to go down a hallway? These characteristics are tied to the materials the architect chooses to define a specific area, and those choices play out in the definition of larger building typologies. A dialogue goes on between the abilities of those building materials (their structural strength, opacity, durability against outside forces) and the activities they hold inside and facilitate. This dialogue has implications for how those activities are carried out and for the interactions of the people using those spaces; it has the potential as well for a rethinking of the very activities themselves. Behaviors associated with an activity are tied directly to the physical properties (transparency, opacity, openings for movement) of the boundary that either links it to or separates it from other activities or contexts. The introduction of material energies into architecture not only opens up opportunities in terms of what materials we build with, but also allows reinterpretations of the activities and events we design for.

What ties auras, comfort control, and material energies together are their shared physical properties: they are all defined by waves, particles, and chemical interactions. What separates them from one another is the extent to which they can perform as a building material. The intention here is to highlight the differences among the three so as to outline a road map by which the physical properties of these auras and comfort controls might be amplified, allowing them to become building materials able to create architecture. This does not call for the elimination of the first two material uses in architectural space, but simply identifies the opportunity for the third to emerge as a design option.

AURAS

The use of the word *atmosphere* in architecture is an attempt to describe a quality of space distinct from the geometries that define the space. It was thought to be first used to describe the gaseous states that surround celestial bodies, having been emitted from the planets,[1] much like the aura of "more than natural" light around a saint's head denoting his or her divine nature. Auras and atmospheres are linked to the object from which they radiate; they are intertwined with other objects that allow the aura either to pass through them or to reflect off of them. To discuss atmosphere in architecture, we simply swap celestial bodies and saintly heads for building surfaces. The architectural critic Jeff Kipnis refers to the relationship between the surface and the effects it helps produce as the "cosmetic." In this formulation, atmospheric qualities rest as surface embellishments, while all implications for broader spatial organization can be traced back to the geometries they exist on. Kipnis describes these cosmetics as "fields, as a blush or shadow or highlight, as *aura* or air... more atmospheres than aesthetic."[2] Kipnis's

AURAS
Ecstasy of Saint Teresa
(1647–1652) by
Gian Lorenzo Bernini

St. Jakob-Park Football
Stadium in Basel (2001)
by Herzog & de Meuron.

essay, "The Cunning of the Cosmetic," was a response to an earlier interpretation of Herzog & de Meuron's work that categorized this aspect of it as ornamental. It's been nearly fifteen years since Kipnis introduced the term, but architectural interest in these atmospheric auras goes back much further. One has to assume it has existed since light from campfires first bounced off of cave walls or sunlight reflected off of a puddle of water to produce patterns on a nearby surface. And the interest continues today, as atmospheric moods and ephemeral effects always accompany architecture, reflecting off, passing through, or emanating out of the surfaces that construct a space. Auras are distinct and yet intangible qualities that hover quite literally on top of the surface.

Auras are in a subordinate relationship with surfaces: the first requires the second. Under such a regime, luminosity from reflections or glows emitted from lit surfaces, temperature gradients emanating from façades, and scent and moisture traces rising from material weathering all rely on a surface to provide a physical boundary. These auras may at times appear interactive (manifesting cause and effect) or immersive (surrounding the body like a cloud of water droplets or a dizzying light display), but they are predominantly theatrics, lacking the critical quality of an architectural building block: they don't take any of the risks associated with defining programmatic activities. As theatrics, they may be layered on top of one another as a means of demonstration, but they always link back to the surface and geometries that are the true architectural materiality of the space. Surface and geometry are the instigators of the effect—remove the surface and the effect is gone. Lift the effect from the constraints of the surface, however, and it becomes a material in and of itself—a material energy.

One of the simplest analogies to show the difference between auras and material energies is a comparison of stucco and concrete. Stucco and concrete look rather similar at first glance; however, one is an application, a finish laid over a structure, and the other is a material with structural properties itself, in this case for spanning distances and for handling loads and forces of compression and stacking. Stucco is simply placed on top of a separate organizational system, while concrete at one time launched a revolution within the building and design industry because of the activities that its malleability and structural spans could accommodate and reinterpret. The distinction between what is applied to a structure and what is structural in itself parallels the distinction between auras and material energies. Although stucco can also act as a weatherproof membrane, which is more than an aura is capable of, the comparison does allow a glimpse of what's at stake if atmospheric effects could do more than act as an appliqué on an existing material system and instead take on roles as primary building materials.

A discussion interested in auras produces only terminologies of intention without a clear directive for the implementation of auras in architecture or, more importantly, for assessing the implications of their use. Using terms such as *atmosphere*, *effect*, or *sensation* to define conditions of interest affords few physical means or notions as to how to quantify, measure, and control them. The means of control are hidden within, layered beneath, and simultaneously acknowledged and overlooked; because of this, auras are relegated to something closer to a desired by-product. As a result, energies (in the form of auras) have been stunted in their growth as potential materials; the architecture discipline has allowed them to remain reliant on constructed surfaces, the current medium of choice, and has never established standards for their use. Defining them as atmospheric qualities implies that such energies carry a minimal amount of responsibility: they don't prevent rain from falling on our heads, they don't provide privacy or control crowds of people, and they don't push back strongly enough against the activities and events that exist around them to inform and control the subsequent spatial organization, either intentionally or accidentally. They are indeed simply "cosmetic."

It is necessary to be clear and show the limited discourse of atmospheric effects for what it is: the result of an extremely conservative definition of architecture that sees all avenues for building space to exist in the geometries and walls alone. Architecture in that light is a profession that defines activities and social constructs, a profession that hones techniques for delineating circulation and passage, a profession that imbues materials with the burden of protecting the individual or object from its surrounding context with surfaces. It follows that the material should be a geometric surface or a solid construction, whether made from transparent glass or opaque concrete, and any aura the architect produces in the design after that is simply an application. An architect today armed with a vocabulary consisting of *glows, shimmers, blushes*, and the like is nurturing a specialization within an already narrow bandwidth of investigation that essentially amounts to the production of special effects. The attraction of producing an elusive godliness—a heavenly, metaphysical experience—is admittedly undeniable. But glows, moods, and effects make one suspicious of them, doubting that they can ever be more than tricks of the eye or simple sensations that flutter across the body, fleeting and ancillary, effects that are incapable of having the strength needed to define and control a physical, architectural boundary.

This could be why so many current architectural proposals in this vein are light-based endeavors relegated to the visual spectrum: light-defined space can be more clearly demonstrated and accessed by the participant. Yet such auras are playing essentially the same role today as they did several hundred years ago. Because these are not materials per se, but seductive by-products that divert our attention from what's doing the real work (even if one believes that such effects are the primary focus of that work), it is still the surface that actually enacts the spatial and organizational strategies of the spaces being defined and created. And no matter how infatuated the architectural discipline is, eloquent adjectives and metaphors will never put auras on the front line, with the materiality to become architecture in their own right. As the delivery systems that either hold these auras or provide the surface for them to exist against continue to advance (via curtain wall construction, form fabrication, and assembly techniques), they allow for new possibilities in the field of architecture. Yet the aura's inability to physically control a territory means it cannot do the same.

COMFORT CONTROL

If auras are the epitome of unassessed intentions, loosely controlled qualities with even slimmer spatial loads, *comfort control* exhibits a precision relative to energy that can be said to falter by virtue of its dedication to reproducing only what we already know to exist: desirable weather. Auras, characterized with poetic hand gestures and vocabulary to describe effects, may never achieve architectural control, but they do aspire to an element of creativity in their ambiguity. Comfort control, on the other hand, is the result of placing energies in the hands of an engineering know-how that seeks to emulate the standards of an ideal climate—temperature, light levels, humidity control—and sees to it that this singular and homogeneous consensus is instilled and propagated in the service of human comfort and product preservation. We've asked little more from it.

The irony is that as technological advancements have provided opportunities to quantify and simulate these energies like never before, they have been used only to better maintain this already predefined endgame: achieving climatic comfort for the body. Visualization software, first developed for the National Aeronautics and Space Association (NASA) space missions and later refined during the United States energy crisis in the 1970s, allows us to see and manipulate these energies in new ways, and we now have mechanical systems to control them with more precision. Yet we view these advancements only as a chance to more efficiently operate the building already designed in geometries and surfaces. This increased knowledge is deployed to refine the architectural forms and masses sketched by the designer with the aim to maximize energy efficiency in delivering this ideal, but not to reconsider how those energies could themselves be amplified or directed in order to pick up some of the spatial loads of the architectural surfaces they're currently in service of.

With comfort as the measuring stick for success, simulating the performance of various energies is seen as a means for reconfiguring the initial forms to increase efficiency, but little else. Architectural forms and surfaces position the activities and programs, while the comfort controls fill the interior. This means that activities have been placed—and spatial organizations and hierarchies already determined—before these energies take on their role, which is to assure that the predefined spatial organizations are comfortable to human senses. They are essentially climatized volumes of already captured spaces.

Comfort control spans an array of variables, from light, temperature, humidity, and scent, to the speed of air moving over the body and the range of sound decibels carried through that air. Architects are probably most familiar with the concept of comfort control as it is presented in the psychrometric chart.

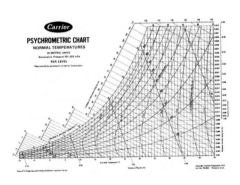

COMFORT CONTROL
Psychrometric Chart.
Attempts to standardize an
ideal comfort level have
led to the control of humidity,
temperature, light levels,
and acoustic energies
for simply replicating ideal
exterior climates on
the interiors of predefined
geometric architectural
forms.

Material Energies

Created by Willis H. Carrier in 1904, this chart has played a formidable role in bracketing the selection of material variables for control in architecture and epitomizes the architect's mind-set when turning to these energies. One could tell a similar story with any of the variables above, but the relationship of temperature and humidity to comfort is most widely documented and apparent in our daily lives.

As a field of engineering and physics, psychrometrics looks to the properties of gas-vapor mixtures in the widest possible sense, dealing essentially with air and water.[3] (Carrier referred to the psychrometric chart as the hygrometric, or humidity-measuring, chart.) The chart built on predecessor tables, specifically in the field of meteorology, where empirical property values including water vapor pressure, barometric pressure, wet bulb, and dry bulb were used for documenting and predicting weather behavior.[4] It was early in the nineteenth century when amateur scientists and enthusiasts began their quest to understand the weather through advancing tools and measuring devices, including developing a vocabulary that bought us the names of the clouds we still use to this day.

The first implementation of psychrometric knowledge in the design of buildings was not so much to control temperature as to control humidity as it pertained to manufacturing, most specifically in cotton and textile factories. Extreme fluctuations of heat and humidity would often cause factories to halt production due to the effect these shifts would have on the materials being produced. At the beginning of the twentieth century, this control of temperature and humidity to assure the quality of goods would expand to include climate controls to attract and provide comfort for people who purchased these very same goods in commercial spaces. As the practice moved to stores and movie theaters, though, an ideal comfort level proved more difficult to define; because it had to take into account the subjective responses of human skin and individual human sensory systems, as opposed to the more easily measured qualities of a product that was being fabricated (such as the tensile strength of cotton on looms), an agreed-upon ideal was elusive.[5]

It should come as little surprise that the guidelines selected and set forth for implementing climate controls were shaped in no small way by the industry that would service them, that of mechanical engineering.[6] The perimeters were defined in an attempt to standardize and fortify a fledgling industry and profession, solidifying its economic and professional role in an ever-expanding sector of business development and convincing its detractors—various city commissions and private "open-air crusaders," to name a few—of its value. The heating and ventilation community knew that to respond to the commissions and state-issued regulations being placed upon them, they themselves would need to provide findings in support of their work. They did so in 1917, convening the American Society of Heating and Ventilating Engineers (ASH&VE) annual meeting with the intention of creating their own data to show the need for mechanical ventilation.[7] Eventually, they developed the Comfort Chart of 1922 to counter dissent from outside the field by defining human comfort level through quantitative methods.

But by defining the comfort ideal of these interior spaces, the Comfort Chart implicitly defined the ideal natural climate of the outdoors as well. Quantifying the ideal temperature, humidity, and air speed levels meant that even the most idyllic vacation spots would be judged against the parameters set forth by these laboratory findings. As Gail Cooper succinctly states, "When natural climate was the ideal, mechanical systems sometimes fell short, but when quantitative standards of human comfort became the measure, natural climate was found wanting.... When no town could deliver an ideal climate, all towns became potential markets for air-conditioning."[8]

As these standards were put in place, they essentially locked down the architectural profession's relationship to these energies; once they had been dictated by engineers, these energies never reached the hands of the architectural designer to become part of a larger creative endeavor. During this fledgling stage, mechanical systems were deployed to retrofit the geometric and spatial configurations of existing buildings. Beyond the design of the air-delivery systems themselves, spatial configurations were considered only in terms of the dichotomy of a conditioned space versus an unconditioned space, and possibly the blur that occurred as one spilled into the other. Today, despite the technological advances of the past several decades, not much has changed in this regard. This is in part because even though the standards followed may change slightly over time, our adherence to a quantitative standard still guides our actions with respect to these energies. The largest obstacle standing in the way of architects engaging these energies is the received knowledge on where innovation exists. Currently, innovation is tracked and defined through the advancements of the technologies that deliver comfort control energies more efficiently. Innovation is not recognized in any approach that allows these energies to subsume some responsibility as a building block material, becoming a way of defining and organizing space and people.

This is a critical point to the discussion, because comfort exists as a known and defined endpoint, the speed and efficiency of the technology that delivers this comfort will always remain the criteria for judging perceived innovations within the field. Solar panels, the ubiquitous green swatches of land on building rooftops, arrays of windmills, red and blue mechanical system diagrams—each acts as a stand-in, a gadget to absorb the calls for advancement within the profession (this will be discussed further in Chapter 4, "The Shape of Energy"). This is because, as design professionals, we're unaware of what to do should we ever have the energy we need. Architecture has overlooked the possibilities of energy becoming a material that is indeterminate and that offers design ambiguity because comfort control as a goal has stayed constant, and the only other place for innovation to read is in the gadgets that can get us there cheaper, faster, and cleaner.

Energy has remained largely in the hands of engineers. If this range of energies is ever to become a material for building space and architecture, it will need to be seen as generative, a means of appropriating, mutating, and bastardizing energy currents, waves, and chemical particles. Until then, maintaining criteria for comfort will only reinforce a fascination with the technology itself that seeks to deliver the specified comfort levels. To make the shift from comfort control to material energies possible, however, it is important to work within the units of measurement tied to these material energies during the design process, to quantify their behaviors and actions through a means that makes the materials workable as new design ideas are explored and refined. The advancements in engineering that brought the comfort control of air-conditioning and heating over the last century have also made these representations and visualization techniques available to the architect.

As architects continue to borrow techniques from adjacent fields to visualize information and materials, including material energies, it raises the question: can architects also adopt other ways of thinking about the material boundaries they operate on during the design phase of a building and its construction? Physicists, for example, define a boundary not as a tangible thing but as an action, and therefore see our environments as energy fields where boundaries operate as transitional states of that field.[9] Boundaries in this case are understood as behaviors that remain variable and so exist only when energy is transitioning in state. As we've already discussed, climate engineers and mete-orologists, like mechanical engineers, have techniques for visual-izing similar gradient conditions of atmospheric pressure, as well as thermal boundaries and air velocity. The important mat-ter here has more to do with understanding the behavioral prop-erties of these energies as we work with them and asking more of them in terms of how they might define and construct spatial boundaries.

Energies currently aren't asked to do more than what they are already known to be able to do: deliver ideal climates and visual effects. This is in part because the architectural discipline is not operating in the units of measurement necessary to work with these material energies, which makes it difficult to engage the potential design innovations tied to the proclivities of the materials' behaviors. At present, the architect sketches through representational techniques and units of measurement that favor solid masses and surfaces, and in turn invents and envisions architectures of great spans or concrete shells of nearly unbelievable thinness, knowing that if the technical issues related to their production can be resolved, the resultant spaces might deliver something unique enough to warrant the efforts needed to explore these materials further. But the vocabulary for energies is not yet at this point.

Michelangelo's St. Peter's Basilica and Le Corbusier's Villa Savoye are constructed with materials harnessed from the resources available on the planet (whether iron ore for steel, or water, lime, and steel for reinforced concrete, or glass and paint), yet these materials don't come together in this architecture in ways that mimic geologically produced cave voids in the earth. Similarly, we should not engage available energy systems, those engineered conditions that fill spatial voids, simply to emulate existing weather or ideal climates. We don't often mistake caves as being architecture, so neither should we confuse material energies with interior comfort controls that seek only to reproduce preconceived climates.

MATERIAL ENERGIES

The boundaries and edges created to give architecture shape operate in an interaction between the material thus deployed and the body's ability to perceive it. How the body perceives that boundary-creating material dictates the type of influence it has on defining and maintaining a space. If material energies are to be deployed to provide architecture with shape, how can the architect design the dictating interactions, in this case between the human body's sensory perceptions and the stimuli in our environment? The answer has two parts. In the following chapter ("Sensorial Envelopes"), I'll discuss the opportunities related to the human body's sensory perception in more detail. The discussion here will focus on the stimuli (electromagnetic, thermal, acoustics, and chemical) and how they can be amplified to become material energies.

Interactions between the human body and the stimuli of the environment can be divided into three types: physical (exerting force on the body), informational (providing way-finding cues), and trophic (metabolic).[10] Distinctions between these three types are not always consistent, and it's not important for a particular set of material energies to be understood exclusively as one type or another. The common air curtain that can be found in supermarkets and stores today, which blows air across a threshold that would otherwise have an aluminum and glass door, can be understood as both a physical as well as an informational interaction. It's physical—it keeps insects and light rain from making their way into the building, but is not forceful enough to keep an individual from passing through it. And it's informational—the air movement, which is mostly imperceptible to the human eye, signals what appears to be an opening in the store façade for an individual to move through. It's unlikely anyone would spend much time directly on the threshold before feeling uncomfortable enough to pick a side, but the force of the air velocity is not strong enough to prevent that movement or misuse. These three types of material energies interact with the human body in ways unique from one another, not only giving a range of variability in how these materials can be deployed, but (as will be shown) also demonstrating capabilities one would assume only solid materials can handle.

Street lighting is probably the clearest example of light deployed as a material energy, engaged with in an informational interaction. The following distinctions that demonstrate how light as material energy differs from the auras or comfort controls already discussed may appear overly simplistic, but they help to affirm the respective characteristics of the three and their potentials for design. The reflections and shimmers that bounce off the walls and surfaces of architecture are *auras,* to be observed either from within (as in an immersion of light) or from a distanced vantage point. Light deployed as *comfort control* can be visually represented prior to its implementation, quantified in units of lumens designed to meet the specifications of a reading room, office space, or lobby; the specifications are calibrated precisely for the comfort of the eyes, and more often than not comprise homogenous light levels reaching from the surface of one wall to the other, sandwiching the program inside. Street lighting, however, uses light as a material energy to manipulate the night into accessible territories, providing both security and a defined area that can reliably be controlled for activities to occur within its boundaries.

The light from an overhead street lamp in a public park has an edge. When you're standing in the light, you have access to information about your environment that is lost when the light goes out or when you step outside its boundary. The boundary of visible light is informational, not physical: you can pass through the boundary it produces. Yet the failure of that street light to work would have consequences for the activities and people gathered in the spaces it provides when it does work. An informational material energy will not suffice for securing boundaries from unwanted individuals or shielding those standing beneath it from inclement weather because it doesn't create a physical contact with the body. It does, however, influence an individual's choice in where they might locate themselves. Street lighting may share characteristics with auras, but the shimmers, glows, and blushes that sweep across and emanate from translucent building skins are, by contrast, accountable for very little! Ask yourself this: has an aura that fails to work ever had any meaningful consequence? Has an atmospheric effect laid across a surface ever undermined the surface's primary role?

Street lighting doesn't simply recreate the natural lighting of the sun. In an attempt to bring light to the night, it instead gives us hundreds of thousands of small point sources directly over our heads. At times these stand independently, as an isolated circle of light in a dark urban field, and at other times they flood together along linear tracks, like paths and roads, or pool together in large public forums, like stadiums and parks. This conglomeration of individual light sources produces an electric gradient that appears to flow between and around the static structures also present, often binding them together in familiar and unfamiliar ways. It can either reinforce existing connections seen during the light of day (streets and highways) or produce altogether new hierarchies of movement and circulation in parks and plazas that do not exist when the sun is out. The size of these "washes" of street lighting may appear as large as an entire metropolis (or maybe even two or three, connected by a collection of electric threads). Alternatively, with just a peripheral glance to the outer edges of the dark expanses, one might see smaller discrete moments of connectivity between a single structure and its adjacent garden or path.

Light and heat were at one point thought to be inseparable when fire was the only option for producing light. Over time the two were separated as the science behind them was better understood. Light improved in the qualities it possessed, including brightness and color, as well as in terms of the safety of those around it, progressing from smoldering embers left on ledges, to the burning of oils and gases in lamps, to the glowing of metals in incandescent bulbs, and eventually to the Light Emitting Diodes (LEDs) of today. Light also went through a transformation in the successive responsibilities assigned to it, moving from illuminating the interiors of buildings, where it was once kept

A BASIC MATERIAL ENERGY
Street lighting acts as a simple example of how a *material energy* distinguishes itself from climate controls or auras. The physical boundaries and edges of space it creates within otherwise dark expanses shape pockets of light that facilitate commerce and social encounters that would otherwise not occur at that particular time of night.

in central hearths or carried by hand, to lighting the perimeter edges of buildings, and finally making its way into streets as free-standing street lights, producing its own shapes in open fields and plazas with interiors (though singular) of its own.[11] Street lighting is but a beginning point to the development of an array of additional material energies, working in unison to build a new architecture.

DEVELOPMENTS IN MATERIAL ENERGIES

Much of the human effort to acquire territorial control over our surroundings can be discussed through the control of light over the last four centuries alone. But the human body has recently found itself in new territories beyond Earth, which has required the achievement of something far more ambitious than the mere replacement of a spectrum of radiation (visible light) lost as

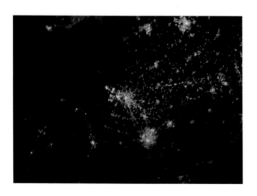

URBAN WASH
Photograph of Antwerp, Belgium, at night shot from the NASA International Space Station.

the sun disappears daily because the Earth is rotating on an axis. When the Apollo astronauts traveled to walk on the moon, they were the only humans to ever move beyond the Earth's natural "force field"—the magnetosphere.[12] This protective zone is formed by a magnetic field generated by the Earth itself that extends into space, protecting the planet as it deflects the worst of the sun's radiation out to space.[13] Anyone traveling beyond this protective zone is subject to cosmic rays that originate beyond our solar system as well as radiation from our sun known as "energetic particles," which can cause sickness and possible death after exposure over long periods of time (or even over shorter periods of time during intense solar flares).

The astronauts of the Apollo mission who went to the moon were gone for roughly ten days and were lucky not to have been in space during a major eruption on the sun, which would have threatened them with dangerous levels of radiation. Though the International Space Station is within Earth's magnetosphere, it still has a special thick-walled room that astronauts can retreat to during such solar storms. If astronauts in the future intend to travel further and for longer times, they will need radiation shielding. But the production of a shielded spacecraft enclosed in a level of protection equal to that singular room on the space station is unlikely due to the increased mass involved, and the expense and difficulty in getting those materials into space. For that reason, some believe it's worth investing instead in producing a portable magnetosphere, much like Earth's, to surround the spacecraft.[14]

Researchers at the Rutherford Appleton Laboratory—operated by the Science and Technology Facilities Council—at the

University of York, Strathclyde, and the Instituto Superior Técnico, Lisbon, have undertaken experiments to show that it is possible to "scatter" dangerous levels of radiation heading toward a spacecraft with a portable magnetosphere. The portable magnetosphere would be created by producing a cloud of charged particles of protons and electrons, known as a plasma cloud, that would surround the spacecraft. To prevent the plasma cloud from dissipating, a charged wire mesh would wrap the craft, holding the cloud in place.[15] The team plans to fly a test satellite protected by such a plasma cloud in space. The experiment has a predecessor: in 1984, during a mission called Active Magnetosphere Particle Tracer Explorer (AMPTE), an attempt was made to study the physics of plasma by surrounding a satellite with a plasma cloud one thousand kilometers across. That mission, though, had no way of containing the plasma, and it simply drifted away over time. The plasma clouds for the latest spacecrafts would be roughly one hundred meters wide in order to influence the direction of the unwanted radiation and cosmic rays. It offers a unique demonstration of the possibilities of shaping and holding a complex layer of deployed energy.

It's not necessary to look to satellites and spacecraft to find other examples of harnessed material energies currently in use today, though they appear mostly in the form of devices at the product scale. As with light, distinctions can be shown in how sound waves as material energy differ from auras or comfort controls, and so present new potentials for design. The tranquil sounds of running water in courtyards or choreographed vibrations from an art installation are auras, providing a sensory lulling of sound, tantalizing to the ears. The control of decibels through the shape of a theater's interior configuration, which occurs through the addition of panels that either dampen or redirect sound waves, is associated with comfort control as it pertains to the ear. This is an attempt to optimize the reception of the music being performed for the spectator, yet it limits the architecture that is created to do so. The human ear can hear frequencies from roughly 20 Hz to 20,000 Hz, but this doesn't prevent us from working with frequencies we can't hear that affect the human body in other ways, including through the skin of our bodies, which can detect frequencies that are roughly around 2 to 14 Hz. We can also use sound waves as material energies by deploying audible sound wave frequencies to mask or cancel other existing sound waves within geographically precise coordinates for separating zones of activity.

For example, sound was manipulated and deployed as a spatial material at the 2008 US Republican National Convention. Convention organizers used two acoustic devices that funneled sound waves to individuals through highly focused audio beams,

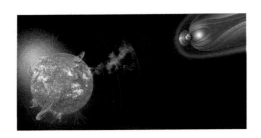

EARTH'S MAGNETOSPHERE
Artist illustration of events on the sun changing the conditions in Near-Earth space.

acting much like spotlights. With such devices, "a multiplicity of speakers are phased so sound that would normally go off to the side or up or down, cancels out, while sound directly in front is reinforced."[16] The Long Range Acoustic Device (LRAD) was used to convey directions and information over long distances (nearly four blocks away) in a clear, calm voice, either pinpointed like a rifle scope to an individual or opened into a broader cone. A similar device, the Hypersonic Sound (HSS), was used as a display system at the convention to play past speeches by presidents in tightly controlled beams: viewers could simply step into and out of the display to listen. If a visitor moved his or her head six inches to the side in either direction away from the beam, the sound would disappear completely. This technology is not unique to governments and political organizations, but is also used in offices, allowing multiple people to work in close proximity without requiring drywall partitions to counter the volume from nearby televisions and presentations occurring in adjacent spaces. In other instances, sound can be used for crowd control: the LRAD, when weaponized, can generate sound levels capable of producing nausea and pain in the individual target, and is most commonly used at sea as an anti-pirate device or by the US military in hostile territory to repel individuals or crowds.

Somewhat more architectural uses of sound as a material energy have emerged in unexpected venues. In Barry, South Wales, when teenagers loitering outside of grocery stores became a disturbance to owners and shoppers alike, a member of the town took it upon himself to create a device that emitted a high frequency heard only by younger individuals in an attempt to drive them away. As humans age, our abilities to hear higher frequencies deteriorate, and Howard Stapleton took advantage of that bit of information to settle on a 17.4 kHz frequency as one that he believed nearly no one over thirty would be able to hear, and nearly anyone under twenty would.[17] Without causing any damage to the hearing of the loitering teenagers, the broadcast frequency made the perimeter of the store irritating enough that the kids didn't want to be there any longer. In doing so, the store produced a visually transparent edge that no one could see and only a specified age demographic could perceive.

The growing awareness of the material energies' capabilities when harnessed allows for speculations on future spatial strategies. When the materials are seen in terms of decision-making techniques, architectural design agendas can expand. Commercially available discrete products, like some of the sound devices described above, only reinforce the mentality of product-to-problem solutions, in which individual material energies are assigned to individual sensory perceptions (light for the eyes, sound for the ears): street lighting, for example, is tied to the visible spectrum of light that our eyes can detect, defining a boundary edge within a darkened context. But energy systems can also be amplified and controlled to build architecture by creating a thickened integration of several material energies on top of one another, demarcating territories in gradient formations. Working together, they can more strongly define boundary edges, making them capable of supporting additional activities beyond what light can do alone, for example. Similar to how a combination of Portland cement, aggregate, water, and steel provides us with reinforced concrete for spans of floors and ceilings, the potential combinations and integrations of multiple material energies layered on top of one another offer intriguing possibilities. Just as techniques of providing light in the evenings in no way intend to—or can—reproduce the sun, this growing list of materials will produce an architectural and urban design far more open-ended and robust for the architectural profession than the act of mimicking could ever provide.

Whether material energies are electromagnetic, sound waves, or thermodynamics, their physical properties consist of waves and particles. The behavioral properties of material energies as well as the techniques for representing them cannot be understood as lines and surfaces, but must be seen as gradients—an alternative definition of a physical boundary that will, in turn, inform alternatives to the aesthetics, shapes, and typologies of space. Robin Evans reminds us that the strategies we use to divide space simultaneously play a role in how we as inhabitants are brought back together, with implications for our social organization. Material energies have the potential to reshape the geographic sites with which they share their physical makeup, redefining what constitutes an architectural space as well as the programs within that space. The resultant spatial constructions and professional reconfigurations will shape the worlds we seek to create in far-reaching ways—socially, economically, and politically. And it begins with a very simple yet fundamental shift in our definition of an architectural boundary.

1 Mark Wigley, "The Architecture of Atmosphere," *Daidalos* (June 1998), 18.

2 Jeff Kipnis, "The Cunning of Cosmetics," in *El Croquis 60+84: Herzog & De Meuron 1981-2000* (Madrid: El Croquis, 2005), 26.

3 Donald P. Gatley, "Psychrometric Chart Celebrates 100th Anniversary," *ASHRAE Journal* (November 2004), http://www.handsdownsoftware.com/Psychrometrics-100th-Bday.pdf. (accessed 20 October 2012).

4 Ibid.

5 Gail Cooper, *Air-Conditioning America: Engineers and the Controlled Environment, 1900-1960* (Baltimore: John Hopkins University Press, 1998), 82, 102.

6 Ibid., 51.

7 Ibid., 68.

8 Ibid., 79.

9 D. Michelle Addington and Daniel L. Schodek, *Smart Materials and New Technologies: For the Architecture and Design Professions* (London: Architectural Press, 2004), 7.

10 David B. Dusenbery, *Sensorial Ecology, How Organisms Acquire and Respond to Information* (New York: W.H. Freeman and Company, 1992), 10.

11 Matthew Luckiesh, *Artificial Light: Its Influence Upon Civilization* (Ulan Press, 1923), 154.

12 "New Spaceship Force Field Makes Mars Trip Possible," Science and Technology Facilities Council, http://www.stfc.ac.uk/RALSpace/Areas+of+expertise/Space+Research/Mini+magnetospheres/In+the+news/24654.aspx (accessed 4 May 2013).

13 "Shield for the Starship Enterprise: A Reality?," Rutherford Appleton Laboratory, 19 April 2007, http://www.spaceref.com/news/viewpr.html?pid=22415 (accessed 4 May 2013).

14 Ibid.

15 "deflector shield," The Encyclopedia of Science, http://www.daviddarling.info/encyclopedia/D/deflector_shield.html.

16 Amanda Onion, "Weapon Grade Sound," Facts Are Facts, http://www.facts-are-facts.com/news/sne-201204-sound.ihtml (accessed 20 October 2012).

17 Sarah Lyall, "Rowdies Buzz Off as the Mosquito Bites," *The Age* (Melbourne), 30 November 2005, http://www.theage.com.au/news/world/rowdies-buzz-off-as-the-mosquito-bites/2005/11/29/1133026467657.html (accessed 16 February 2008).

The hollow mound is located on top of an existing city infrastructure grate, trapping excess heat and conducting it onto the surface, making the space available for people to recline upon and gather around.

Heat is also redirected from the mound to multiple smaller, flat zones that include a table and set of chairs; these zones are tightly configured to trap and maintain surface and air temperatures up to several feet above the ground.

SIRENUSE, 2011
Model
Sean Lally WEATHERS

Silicone rubber nubs permit light to move through the form, which still remains soft enough to recline upon.

Wire heating elements are embedded in aluminum-filled polyurethane liquid plastic to produce low thermal levels that can be felt against the body as it reclines on the exterior carpet.

SHAGG, 2009–2010
Prototype
Sean Lally WEATHERS

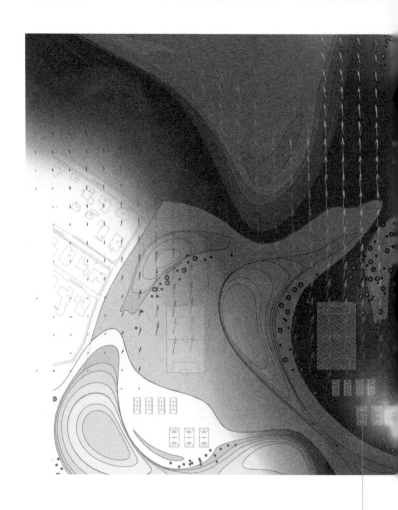

Geo-thermal energy is fed into the soil,
allowing for year-round vegetation growth
and recreational activities.

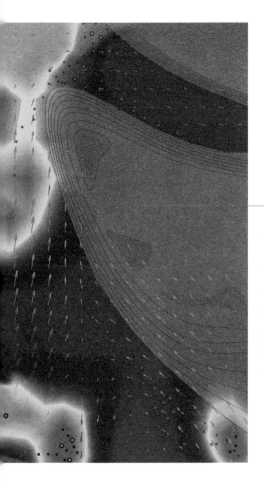

New artificial landforms surround the site perimeter. Built by piling earth on new parking structures and then adding proposed buildings on top of them, the mounds rise on either side in the shape of a valley, tied together by a "climatic wash" that acts as a connecting tissue between the north and the south of the site.

VATNSMYRI URBAN PLANNING, 2007
Site Plan Detail
Sean Lally WEATHERS

Each of the six vitrines located in the garden is identical in its geometric shape, but unique in its interior environment. Each contains a water basin with fluorescent tracer dye, heating systems within the water basin, lighting to detect the fluorescent dyes, fans to direct air currents, and vegetation.

One of the six units was used as a control. Left without any of the applied devices and activated solely by the existing environmental and climatic conditions, this unit was used to gauge the augmented performance of the other five.

AMPLIFICATION, 2006–2007
Sean Lally WEATHERS

The inside surfaces of the acrylic vitrines are etched so as to trap condensation, allowing the water to pool in specified areas.

Fluorescent tracers have been added to the water in the basin and fluorescent lighting is used to track differences in how water, humidity, and air movement and speed are controlled in the different vitrines.

AMPLIFICATION, 2006–2007
Sean Lally WEATHERS

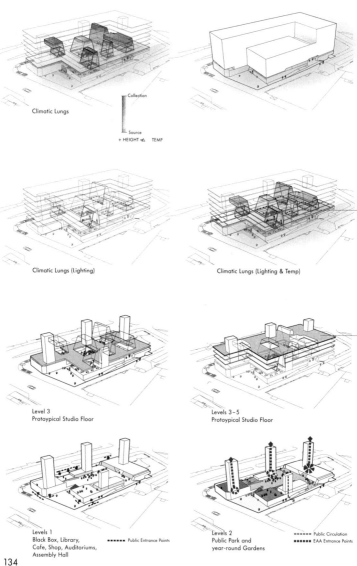

Climatic Lungs

Collection

Source

+ HEIGHT   TEMP

Climatic Lungs (Lighting)

Climatic Lungs (Lighting & Temp)

Level 3
Protoypical Studio Floor

Levels 3 – 5
Protoypical Studio Floor

Levels 1
Black Box, Library,
Cafe, Shop, Auditoriums,
Assembly Hall

■■■■■ Public Entrance Points

Levels 2
Public Park and
year-round Gardens

■■■■■ Public Circulation
■■■■■ EAA Entrance Points

Each of the six "lungs" provides full-spectrum lighting to counteract the short daylight hours of winter. For close to a third of the year, the light source for both the park below and the interiors above comes not from the sky, but from the illuminated "lung" system.

The six "lungs" are organizational systems in the building mass of the upper floors, anchoring the positions of the design studios.

ESTONIAN ACADEMY OF ARTS, 2008
Organizational Diagrams
Sean Lally WEATHERS

WANDERINGS, 2008–2010
Prototype
Sean Lally WEATHERS

Vacuum-formed PETG, a clear polyethylene plastic, is used to create a sealed air cavity containing a heat wire filament that warms the trapped air.

The heat produced by the clear plastic shapes can be engaged by either directly sitting on one of the units, or by walking between a group of the units as heat radiates into the surrounding soil and air.

WANDERINGS, 2008–2010
Prototype
Sean Lally WEATHERS

Acting on the ground plane, the project creates multiple spatial zones from discrete objects that are aggregated based on the radii of the material energies.

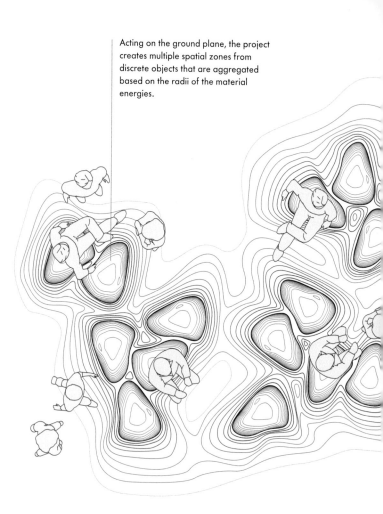

Each piece might be thought to be rather minimal in its production of increased thermal energy but when the units aggregate, they have the potential to make sizable changes to the local microclimates.

WANDERINGS, 2008–2010
Site Plan
Sean Lally WEATHERS

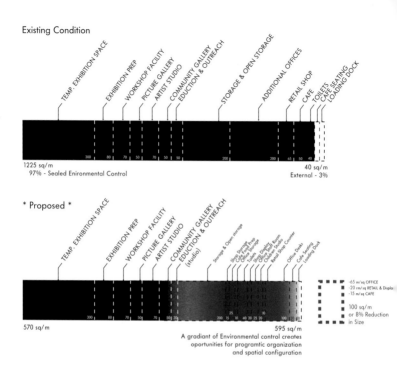

Existing Condition

TEMP. EXHIBITION SPACE
EXHIBITION PREP
WORKSHOP FACILITY
PICTURE GALLERY
ARTIST STUDIO
COMMUNITY GALLERY
EDUCATION & OUTREACH
STORAGE & OPEN STORAGE
ADDITIONAL OFFICES
RETAIL SHOP
CAFE
TOILETS
CAFE SEATING
LOADING DOCK

300 80 70 50 70 50 50   200   200 65 50 40

1225 sq/m
97% - Sealed Environmental Control

40 sq/m
External - 3%

* Proposed *

TEMP. EXHIBITION SPACE
EXHIBITION PREP
WORKSHOP FACILITY
PICTURE GALLERY
ARTIST STUDIO
COMMUNITY GALLERY
EDUCATION & OUTREACH
(studio)
Storage & Open storage
Shop Storage
Exhibition Prep
Office Storage
Toilets
Shop Display
Office Small Room
Children Studio
Retail Shop Counter
Office Desks
Cafe Seating
Loading Dock

300 80 70 50 50 30   200 15 10 40 20 20 20   10   100 120 80

570 sq/m

595 sq/m
A gradient of Environmental control creates
oportunities for programtic organization
and spatial configuration

-65 m/sq OFFICE
-20 rm/sq RETAIL & Display
-15 m/sq CAFE

100 sq/m
or 8% Reduction
in Size

Top: Museum activities are organized along a spectrum of artificial environmental
control. These range from the most closely controlled and least variable (exhibition spaces,
exhibition preparation, galleries) to those with a broader bandwidth of variability (coffee
shop, office desks and spaces, children's studios).

Bottom: This reordered spectrum re-informs the social and organizational patterns
associated with how people use the museum, not by reinventing the specifications and
requirements of the museum, but by reorganizing those same activities using the inherent
properties of the gradient and layered material energies.

CHELTENHAM MUSEUM ADDITION, 2007
Program Diagrams
Sean Lally WEATHERS

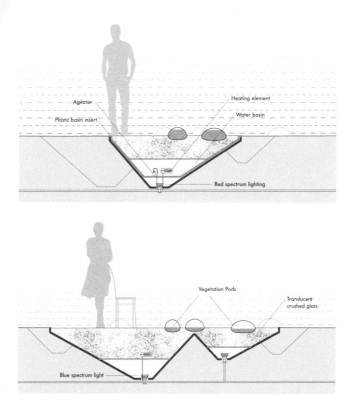

The energy sources of these gradient zones are submerged beneath a layer of rolled crushed glass, which serves to reflect light and disperse water vapor to the spaces above. Because the system is flush with the ground plane, furniture placement and pedestrian movement can occur freely above, organized and dispersed according to the intensities of each designed zone and the desire of the individual to engage it.

UNDERTOW, 2009–2010
Sections
Sean Lally WEATHERS

CHELTENHAM MUSEUM ADDITION, 2007
Model
Sean Lally WEATHERS

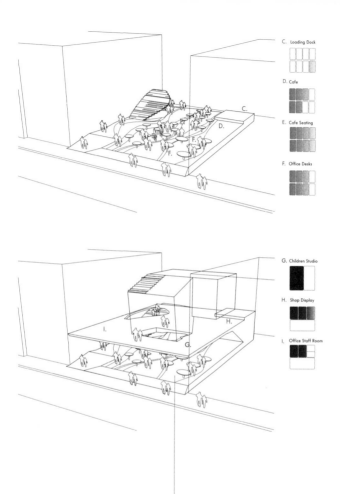

C. Loading Dock

D. Cafe

E. Cafe Seating

F. Office Desks

G. Children Studio

H. Shop Display

I. Office Staff Room

Lifting the museum addition off the first floor
opens the main plaza level in order to
connect the streets on both sides of the site.
Activities associated with a café, seating,
and offices are controlled on this extended
yet spatially conditioned area.

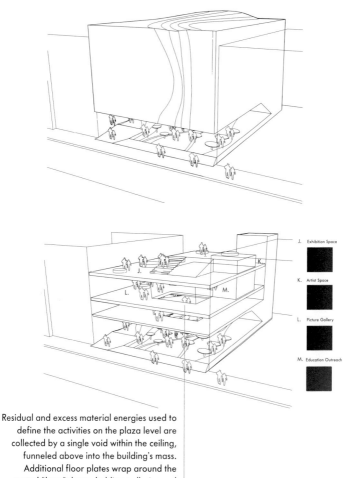

J. Exhibition Space

K. Artist Space

L. Picture Gallery

M. Education Outreach

Residual and excess material energies used to
define the activities on the plaza level are
collected by a single void within the ceiling,
funneled above into the building's mass.
Additional floor plates wrap around the
central "lung" shape, holding galleries and
exhibition halls.

CHELTENHAM MUSEUM ADDITION, 2007
Organizational Diagrams
Sean Lally WEATHERS

SENSORIAL ENVELOPE

The environments that our bodies move within hold more
material stimuli than we are currently able to perceive. Increasing
our ability to detect the gradient fluctuations of *material energies*
used for defining space creates the potential to have a broader
range of boundary edges at the disposal of the architect and the
inhabitant. The means by which we detect difference are the
means by which we make choices about how we engage with the
spatial configurations around us. We currently shape architecture
in relation to the form of the human body's outermost layer.
Our skin is seen as a protective wrap that defines the body's
shape. In turn, the measurements and proportions of the outer
contour calibrate an architecture produced of the surfaces,
skins, and shells that envelop and enclose it. The *sensorial envelope* is a different calibration device for defining architectural
shape that takes into account the body's increased sensitivity to
layered and multiple sensory perceptions, permitting the detection
of our surrounding environments with new lenses and greater
levels of interaction. The human body's engagement with its
material surroundings is becoming more robust due to a range
of technological advancements currently occurring outside
the discipline of architecture, which include both pharmaceutical
enhancements to our central nervous system and brain as well
as implants to improve our existing senses of sight and hearing.
Sensorial envelopes comprise a quantifiable series of sensory
perceptions for detecting and defining the shape of space.

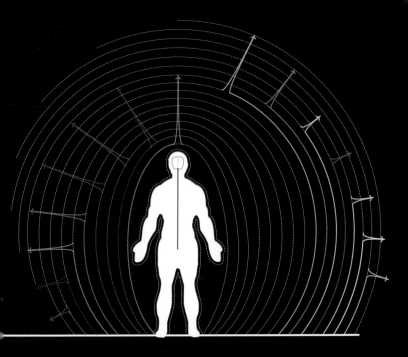

HUMAN SENSES

- Vision
- Audition
- Taste
- Olfaction
- Thermoception (detection of changes in temperature)
- Proprioception (awareness of relative position of body parts in space)
- Nociception (pain sensing)
- Equilibrioception (balance)

INTEROCEPTION
Senses found within the body that involve sensory receptors in internal organs.

ARTIFICIAL SENSES
(analogous to human senses)

- Vision
- Taste
- Olfaction

ARTIFICIAL SENSES
(seen in other species)

- Echolocation (sonar)
- Electroreception (detection of electric fields)
- Magnetoception (detection of Earth's magnetic field)
- Vibrational

CENTRAL NERVOUS SYSTEM
- Pharmaceutical

ARMS RACE

There is a reciprocal relationship evolving between the growing range of materials (*material energies*) that the architect is able to control and the increase in our body's sensory perception (*sensorial envelopes*) due to advances in chemistry and bio-engineering. Because of this duality, neither the environment nor the human body can be seen as the architect's baseline for accommodating the other. Instead, the two are intertwined in their respective developments. The potential exists for an "arms race" that stimulates a reciprocal feedback relationship between the direction of the advancements occurring in material energies and our body's increasing ability to sense them. If neither is seen as static, then neither can be understood as a base condition that informs the other. As we speculate on future architectural spaces, both the materials we use to define physical boundaries as well as the sensory perceptions of the human body that detect them should be assumed to be variables for the architect to engage and question.

INCREASED KNOWLEDGE OF THE BODY

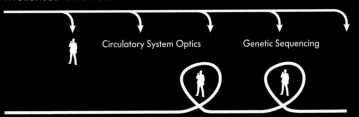

Circulatory System Optics   Genetic Sequencing

INCREASED MATERIAL CONTROL

Mediation and   Protection for
Environmental   Exploration in
Controls   Space or Deep
                       Ocean

INCREASED SENSORY PERCEPTION

ADVANCEMENTS OF MATERIAL ENERGIES

PROFESSIONAL SLIDE RULER

A rather fundamental question arises: if you can meet the needs of a new café, city library, or office space without the use of the surface armatures we've come to know (walls and roofs), would the result be architecture? Distinctions between the professions of architecture and landscape architecture (among others) are less about the difference in materials used than the activities that each is capable of or that we expect it to be able to accommodate. On one end of the spectrum is architecture and its construction of operating rooms or black box theaters that require a level of control not thought possible without that profession's geometries and interiors. On the other end of the spectrum is landscape architecture with its recreational fields, gardens, and plazas that use lighting, vegetation, and roof structures to mediate local climates. If, however, *material energies* can be amplified and controlled so as to accommodate a growing range of activities generally thought to be either outside the scope of landscape architecture or within the scope of architecture—only without the walls and surfaces we associate with defining architecture's form— then we erode an artificial distinction between professions as well as unnecessary dichotomies that stifle design innovation.

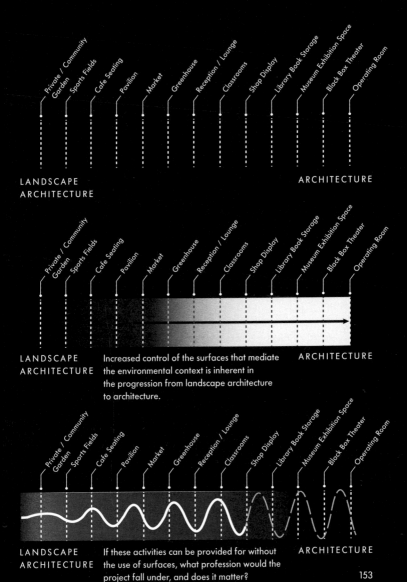

LANDSCAPE
ARCHITECTURE

ARCHITECTURE

LANDSCAPE
ARCHITECTURE

Increased control of the surfaces that mediate
the environmental context is inherent in
the progression from landscape architecture
to architecture.

ARCHITECTURE

LANDSCAPE
ARCHITECTURE

If these activities can be provided for without
the use of surfaces, what profession would the
project fall under, and does it matter?

ARCHITECTURE

153

SENSORIAL ENVELOPES

Our planet offers essentially the same playing field for all creatures that inhabit it.[1] Earth's atmospheric and chemical compositions, though they vary in intensity from locale to locale, are identical around all creatures, whether or not they have the ability to perceive them. What you don't see, still exists. The bee, for example, is capable of seeing ultraviolet light to find pollen concentrations on flowers; the snake hunts warm-blooded mammals at night by detecting variations in infrared light (thermal radiation); some fish can hunt their prey by distinguishing changes in the water's electrical field; and insects communicate with each other through vibrations in vegetation. Each one of these creatures may very well occupy simultaneously a given vicinity, each operating independently from the others because its decision-making tactics are based on differing sensory perceptions. The same environment is "seen" through different lenses, with each creature detecting and inhabiting different spatial organizations embedded within that area. The sensory perceptions of any given creature—its ability to sense a rate of change in its surroundings and therefore make decisions about its own movement in that setting—can make the same locale unique from one creature to the next.

The analogy of a bubble helps to illustrate the spatial zones that keep one animal species or insect distinct from another. Jakob von Uexkull describes such a bubble as containing all the variables accessible to a particular animal in an environment: "as soon as we enter into one such bubble, the previous sur-roundings of the subject are completely reconfigured.... a new world arises in each bubble."[2] The sensory perception of the human body creates a type of interiority that the body resides in, lodged among the surrounding context, because the select amount of information it is capable of detecting is only part of a much larger spectrum. Human sensory perception operates at a particular frequency, making some information about our surroundings apparent while suppressing others. Because the human body's senses operate at frequencies that differ from, say, those of a bumblebee, we experience our surroundings differently from a bee. The human body perceives a flower in terms of its color, shape, and smell, while a bee sees a gradient concentration of pollen at the center of the flower through its infrared sight.

If energy is understood in terms of its capacity to do work, then information is understood according to its ability to organize systems.[3] In order for various energies in the environment to be useful as information, the body needs to be able to perceive them. Our surroundings do not suffer from a lack of such information coursing through them; the issue is more that humans are not always able to sense that distinct material and act upon the information it contains. Technologically speaking, scientists have the ability to visualize and document each of the sensory examples mentioned above through various recording devices and software simulations. What the human body itself lacks is the ability to detect a large swath of those same variables through personal and constant sensory perception. This essentially removes us from a large portion of the very territories we already occupy. Being able to quantify and control a material is only as useful as the information that it can convey to the body for making decisions, from navigation to judging aesthetic values. Because organisms, including the human body, obtain information externally through their senses in order to respond more rapidly to environmental conditions, the question arises as to what strategies are available to locate that additional information currently unavailable to us and how the human body might go about developing those strategies into additional or heightened senses.

For now, we rely so heavily on vision and touch that it is logical to construct building envelopes much like the skin's outer edge. With visually perceivable edges and tactile boundaries, the skin-like envelopes of current architecture are logical outgrowths of this abstraction of the body. But our bodies are also capable of perceiving gradient energy changes, both from a

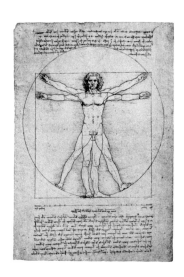

LEONARDO DA VINCI'S "VITRUVIAN MAN"
The human body is often used as a calibration device for architecture through its proportions of parts and wholes.

distance (discerning zones of difference) as well as from a position engulfed within them. And, as will be discussed in more detail, the human body's sensory perception is currently advancing, which means that the gradient boundaries of the material energies discussed earlier have a counterpart in sensory abilities that can newly perceive the range, intensity, and concentrations of the environment beyond the skin's surface. The materials that define spatial boundaries and the human body's senses that detect those edges can both be conceived as multiple and layered contour gradients. If the human body could change to perceive additional sensory information, its use as a calibration device for architecture would also need to change. Access to additional information in the environment means a body with new *sensorial envelopes* could be used to inform and change architecture's shape.

DEFINING THE BODY'S EDGES

The act of manipulating and controlling materials has always been under the purview of the architect; by contrast, our bodies are understood as a constant, something that we can learn more about so as to calibrate space, but not something that is as malleable as the building materials we work with. The conventions that architects operate within as they pertain to the human body are long lived and not easily eclipsed. These stretch from Vitruvius's analogies of human proportions, to that of the building that the body perceives and occupies in *Ten Books on Architecture*, to Leonardo da Vinci's *Vitruvian Man*, which sought to illustrate graphically what Vitruvius only put into words. Where Vitruvius relied on proportions, characterized by statements such as, "the length of the foot is one sixth of the height of the body," Leonardo's "Vitruvian Man" constructed a contoured silhouette that demonstrated relationships between the various parts of the body visually. What we see in the "Vitruvian Man" is predominantly the outline of the body, the outer surface of the human form. In creating that outline, Leonardo created a calibration device that used human proportions as an analogy for current knowledge and beliefs regarding the workings of the universe. This increased knowledge of the body was thought capable of being transcribed into architecture of comparable beauty.

The pursuit of the mathematical proportions of the human body for use in architectural form-making and construction is not unique to architecture in the past, but can be found in our more recent times as well. Le Corbusier's *Modulor Man* (1943) not only synthesized two separately used units of measurement,

SENSORY
HOMUNCULUS
A physical model that represents how much brainpower is dedicated to different sensing body parts.

the empirical system (feet and inches) and the French metric system, but also sought to define a relation between the body's form and nearly all designed objects that came into either physical contact with or eyeshot of that body—from architecture and civil engineering projects to furniture and boats. The human body's outer contour was again tied to height, width, and proportion in a parts-to-whole relationship, which were transcribed to better understand the body's relationship to the objects we use for defining space and holding us. The shape architecture might take was once again believed to be best calibrated to these outer skin contours.

When it comes to how spatial territories are calibrated, which characteristics of our bodies we rely on to engage the physical boundaries we create, it is the outermost layer of the body that architects are traditionally most concerned with. Skin is seen as a protective wrap used to bound the body, producing a quantifiable set of proportions: by measuring the outer skin contour, we can produce ideals for the surfaces, skins, and shells that envelop and enclose the body in architectural form. This is because skin is abstracted as the edge of each individual's physical presence, while architecture is seen to be a body in and of itself, one that reflects the anatomy of its inhabitants like an extended exoskeleton around their collective bodies. Alternatively, these surface materials can work like a fitted or oversized garment for a collected mass, as in the case of tents and tensile structures. In both cases, architects provide apertures, passageways, and room dimensions sized to the proportions of the human body. The shapes of buildings are a response to the outer boundary of the human body for calibrating proportion and scale.

Where Leonardo stopped with soft tissue, muscles, and bones, William Harvey picked up with the circulatory system, and others continued these advancements in knowledge, whether in understanding the optics of the eye in the seventeenth century or developing DNA sequencing in the twentieth century. Architects in turn reflect on this knowledge as it is discovered, asking how it can help inform the body's relationships to the spaces they create. The search for knowledge about the human body's workings continues today.

The human body receives an array of sensory input and uses it to help position itself in a space. This input goes beyond the visual cues most commonly reinforced with surfaces and walls. And these repositioning decisions are often not primary organizational moves, but rather secondary considerations that may vary from one individual to another (moving away from a drafty window, finding a light level best for one's desired activity, or sitting at a preferable distance from a music speaker in a coffee shop). Moreover, the body's various sensory perceptions possess differing degrees of specificity in their ability to perceive stimuli in the environment. They exist in an intriguing, imperfect "in-between": sensitive enough yet not overly sensitive to all the variable change rates in our surroundings.[4] The sensitivity of the body's sensory perception determines what it can identify as boundary limits within the environment and the intensity of the influence that these boundaries will have on the body. The extent to which those edges are identifiable determines how the body distinguishes one shape or threshold from one another.

To understand what sensorial abilities we might be able to intensify requires a clarification of how our senses work. To even determine the number of senses that the human body has depends a lot on how a sense is defined, and there is more debate about this than might immediately be assumed. The general assumption that we have only five senses is likely tied to the fact that five distinct parts of the body can be identified for each of them: the nose, eyes, ears, tongue, and skin. But if senses are defined in terms of different kinds of receptors (nerve endings that respond to a stimulus), then we have about ten. These include vision, hearing, smell, and taste; the skin sense of pressure, temperature, and pain; balance and kinesthesis; and even time.[5] If one wanted to include interoceptive senses (those internal to the body and linked to our organs, such as the pulmonary stretch receptors found in the lungs that control the respiratory rate), then there are an additional six. If senses are gauged in terms of the stimuli to which the body can react, there are about six senses, based on our sensitivity to light, sound, gases, liquids, solids, and body position and motion.[6] These senses transcend the outline of our skin. Even touch, which we associate with the same skin referenced for proportions, can also detect air pressure and wind direction.

Vision is, of course, the most relied upon of our senses, particularly in architecture—for judging distances, the size of a room, and the closeness of others. The proportions of our outer skin surface are relied on so heavily for the judgments, in part because there is a reflexive fear that an emphasis on senses beyond vision will entail a loss of critical awareness. The inherent belief is that this will lead to a "slide into emotional bias in our decision-making criteria, as well as slippage of our intellectual activity."[7] To overcome such instinctual hesitation requires a kind of recuperation of our other senses—an increased engagement, training, and even enhancement.[8] In fact, this type of sensory enhancement is already occurring, ready for architecture to capitalize on.

SENSORY ENHANCEMENT

Examples abound around us that illustrate the current progression and increasing availability of enhanced sensory perception. These include the trajectory from glasses to contact lenses to laser eye surgery; research advancements in immunology for better understanding in correcting the imbalances and attacks on our bodies' immune systems; and pharmaceutical enhancements that supply psychiatric medication to our central nervous system, such as antidepressants, as well as hormonal adjustments, such as testosterone replacement therapy and hormone replacement

AN EVOLUTION
"I was wondering when you'd notice there's lots more steps."
Cartoon by Gahan Wilson,
The New Yorker, July 12, 2004.

during menopause. Nearly all of these enhancements originated in an attempt to correct or heal a condition in those either who were born with a perceived deficiency or who developed an ailment during their lifespan. But what starts out designed for healing inevitably gets reconstituted for performance enhancements in those considered healthy. This includes not only athletes looking to enhance physical performance (through increased body mass, muscle strength, or recovery time), but even those seeking to increase the performance of their minds. A recent poll showed that one in five scientists have used drugs for non-medical reasons to stimulate concentration or memory. These drugs included methylphenidate (Ritalin), which was originally developed for the treatment of attention-deficit hyperactivity disorder, and modafinil (Provigil), generally prescribed for sleep disorders.[9]

Our eyes, ears, and muscles, the physiology of our bodies, are currently developing along a similar trajectory, and we experience many of these advancements in our own heightened sensory perception. The human eye sees a relatively small portion of the electromagnetic spectrum, roughly 400 to 700 nanometers, from purple at the shortest end to red at the longest. It takes instruments of our making to enhance that visible spectrum; infrared cameras, thermal imaging, and x-ray machines permit us to extend perception by converting information that is imperceptible to the body's current sensory system into data that is, often in the form of visual imagery. These enhancing instruments can often get small enough to be absorbed into the body entirely. Corrective glasses were worn outside the body before contact lenses appeared, while in the last two decades surgery has evolved to correct the eye permanently, making even contact lenses unnecessary. Individuals with hearing difficulties associated with increased age once needed to wear devices on the outside of their ears, while today individuals born deaf receive cochlear implants that often allow them to hear for the first time. As this trajectory of artificial sensory advancement continues, one assumes that treatments will eventually be available that grant sensory sensitivity to humans on par with that of insects and other species, including implants to the eyes that increase the visible spectrum to include ultraviolet and infrared light and to the ears that augment human hearing to include higher frequencies.[10]

Augmenting our sensory sensitivity alters how the human body responds to the stimuli in the environment. How the body perceives these stimuli is a process shaped, in large part, by the body's sensory receptors. The more sensitive or numerous these receptors are, the broader the range of stimuli the body can detect. The receptors interact with the stimuli in the environment by detecting specific energies or chemicals and converting that data so that the brain can access it.[11] The way receptors determine how the brain receives information from the environment around the body is a type of translation referred to as *transduction*. The receptor is responsible for transducing the environmental energy into neural signals to be used by the body.[12] When the body sees an object from a distance, energy in the form of light bounces back to the eye through the sense of vision. When an individual bumps into a chair or wall, pressure is placed on the skin and that form of energy is received by the receptors. Chemicals, on the other hand, participate directly in biochemical reactions without needing to be translated by receptors. Instead they interact immediately with the central nervous system.[13]

Sensory perception is not only biological. It also includes an individual's prior experience and cultural biases. Stimuli and receptors are most often discussed in biological terms, as engaged in cause and effect relationships, much like the "trophic" or "physical" forms of material energies discussed earlier, but in fact "informational" stimuli also exist that can be shaped by past experiences or ignored altogether. Architects can culturally shape or manipulate such stimuli on an individual level, based on previous experiences that differ either from one person to the next or, more broadly, from one culture to another.[14] A combination of these three factors—environmental stimuli, physical receptors, as well as cultural and past experiences—informs how individuals detect, respond to, and interact with their surroundings. The discussion here, however, is focused primarily on the relationship between the design of material energies (stimuli) and how the body's sensory perception can be intensified to detect and respond to them. It's specifically this dialogue that offers the availability of new architectural materials to build with, and both are more elastic than we might first assume.

Growing evidence exists that the brain and nervous systems "are in fact not rigid and hardwired but instead plastic and malleable."[15] If specific receptors do not currently exist within the human body, this does not mean the brain and nervous system are incapable of perceiving the signals that an artificial receptor might detect. Within the last decade, a growing number of individuals have sought ways to expand their sensory perception so as to interact with stimuli in the environment that they were not born with the ability to perceive. One example is recent efforts to detect existing electromagnetic fields through the use of magnets surgically inserted under the skin of one's finger. Most people might not be aware how many man-made electromagnetic fields they encounter during the course of their day. These include the 60 Hz electrical field generated by US appliances, the various zones created by a laptop computer's battery location and power supply, and various electrical cords and magnets found around the workplace.[16] It's not that manufacturers are unaware of the electromagnetic fields produced by their devices; it's simply understood that as long as they aren't causing harm to the body, they can and will go largely unnoticed. Other species, however, including some fish, can sense low-frequency electrical fields in the water they swim in and use that perception as a means for hunting prey. This is referred to as electroreception and is prevalent in marine creatures precisely because water conducts the electrical fields to all those living in it better than air. Sharks, for example, likely use electroreception not only to detect prey (because they cannot rely on light, odors, or sound), but also to navigate within ocean currents that produce electrical fields as they pass through Earth's magnetic fields.[17] The awareness of how other species perceive space helps re-inform our knowledge of our environment. So placing a magnet under the skin of the finger is less about accessing something new than it is about perceiving a range of information that already exists.

To access this electromagnetic stimuli, a small magnet is placed under the skin at the tip of the individual's ring finger, where there is a high concentration of nerve density. The ring finger is chosen because it does not usually come into direct contact with objects while grabbing and reaching with the hand. (To give the reader some perspective on the extent to which these experiments take a "do it yourself" approach, individuals trying this also pick this finger because it is the least likely to be missed should something with the experiment ever go wrong.) When the hand enters an electromagnetic field, the individual can feel that field through a "slight oscillation and movement" of the magnet under the skin, which stimulates the somatosensory receptors.[18] These receptor cells are the same ones responsible for perceiving the different aspects of touch, including pressure, temperature, and pain. The magnet does not actually give the user a new sense (physiologically speaking) because it is simply acting against existing receptors. But it does provide an ability to perceive stimuli through the body's existing sensory perception that would otherwise go unnoticed.

Both of these examples—marine animals' electroreception and the self-placed magnet in the ring finger—have to do with what is referred to as passive sensing. This simply means that the sensory perception responds to existing information in the environment. The shark or the human hand does not produce an electrical field; it can only detect when one exists. For the shark, electroreception is an evolutionary trait, while for the human, it is a product of simple curiosity. There are, however, examples of perception that involve active sensing, or "sounding," which is the act of sending out a stimulus in order for it to return to the sender and provide knowledge as to how the environment altered it—in other words, to gather information about that context.[19] This includes the echolocation used by bats and dolphins, which send out high-frequency sounds that then return to the animal, allowing it to judge the distance and location of prey. Humans also use artificial techniques of "sounding," including radar and even flashlights. In the case of a flashlight, light is emitted from the device in the hand, and as it bounces off objects and returns to the eyes of the individual carrying the flashlight, it provides information about the surrounding space. (Standing in an open field at night with a flashlight pointed at the sky grants little information about one's surroundings because nothing is present for that light to bounce back from.) In the case of radar, high-frequency radio waves are sent out and the time it takes for that signal to return is registered. This provides information about the distance of an object from the source. For the information from radar to be useful, though, it needs to be translated

SENSORIAL ADVANCEMENTS
Corrective surgeries and the use of pharmaceuticals have progressed from simply striving to repair sensory deficiencies to levels of recognized averages, and are currently capable of exceeding those abilities.

into visual data that the human eye can interpret on screens and monitors, i.e., the information obtained by radar is useful and accessible only because it can be converted to meet an existing type of sensory perception, usually visual.

Experiments by Kevin Warwick, a scientist and professor of cybernetics at the University of Reading, have sought to find out if the human nervous system and brain are capable of detecting and processing sensory information that they have not been exposed to previously. He was interested not in piggybacking the vibrations of a magnet, say, onto existing receptors, but in bypassing the receptors altogether. Instead of converting additional sensory information to be read by existing sensory systems, as with radar, thermal imaging and x-rays, Warwick was specifically interested in "feeding these signals directly onto the human nervous system in an attempt to bypass our normal human sensory input."[20]

In seeking extra-sensory input, Warwick produced an experiment that included surgically implanting a MicroElectrode Array (MEA) into the "median nerve fibres" of his left arm. The MEA is a device that can either send or obtain neural signals, acting as an interface between neurons in the body and outside electronic circuitry. In this case, the array was connected to an external computer that would send signals, making the array a receptive neural interface. Ultrasonic sensors connecting back to the computer were placed on the rim of a hat that Warwick wore. He was then blindfolded, and as he moved around the room, the sensors on his hat stimulated his nervous system, pulsing when he came near an object and remaining silent when no objects were in the vicinity.

What Warwick found was that it took very little time (just a few minutes) for him to learn the process, but it took several weeks for the brain to recognize accurately the signals being "injected."[21] This is because the sensory input was recognized as a new form of sensory input and not as familiar touch or pressure (as with the stimulus of a magnet under the skin of a finger moving against the somatosensory receptor). Instead, because the array was placed against nerve endings in his arm, the brain made a direct link between the signals that were being received via the MEA and their correlation to the existence or absence of nearby objects. In other words, by bypassing existing receptors of the body, the signals from the sensors on the hat went directly to the central nervous system and on to the brain where they were interpreted and learned. Those new signals provided information about the environment that current sensory receptors (Warwick's eyes were blindfolded) were incapable of interpreting. In return, a new sense was produced.

The sensory abilities discussed above, no matter how peculiar and whether demonstrated in other species or through artificial enhancement, are based on accessing real and quantifiable physical energy. This information exceeds subjective interpretations, and the measurable and controllable variables comprising that information can be sculpted to inform the actions of those that perceive them. Our current sensory traits evolved because they were probably essential for hunting, navigating, and reproduction, but they are now also responsible for dictating how people can be spatially organized. The artificial enhancement of sensory perception means that strategies available to organize people via architecture are also potentially changing.

Increasingly the human body has access to additional information already present; that stimuli only needs greater control to be deployed as a material for architecture.

Because the physical properties of material energies are characterized as gradient thresholds of intensities and fallouts, the body must develop a reciprocal characteristic—that is, a growing awareness of the gradients in its sensory perceptions—to encourage a dialogue with those energies. This dialogue is, of course, key to the ability to define new material edges that can then be recognized and interacted with to produce spatial organizations and shapes. These shapes are a result of the negotiation between our body's sensory perception and the material energies used to define them, producing individual as well as shared experiences.

The outline of the human body used for calibrating spatial boundaries in the case of material energies is not a single line, one that represents the body's outer skin surface alone (in terms of proportion, ergonomics, and juxtapositions), but a multilayered series of sensory edges that extend beyond the skin. These sensorial envelopes are tuned to detect the gradient intensities of the material energies that the architect controls and shapes. They are capable of being individually calibrated based on their varying (and advancing) degrees of specificity as they extend beyond the skin of the body, obtaining information and detecting changes in our environment. This dialogue between the body's sensorial envelopes and the material energies defining a shape provides an ability to locate oneself in relation to the material field one is embedded in and to use that locating function for circulation, movement, and the detection of spatial configurations and hierarchies.

Our body's interaction with material energies produces a type of sensory contact—not merely a tactility, which would presume a coalescing of our senses into that of touch alone, but an overall communication between the body and the stimuli in the environment. Efforts to foster that interaction include both heightening existing sensory receptors of the body to perceive a broader range of sensitivity (those that respond to temperature, pressure, pain, light, sense of position, and the chemical stimuli that come in contact with the nervous system), as well as making advancements in artificial sensory perception that might be analogous to those of other species.

RECIPROCAL DESIGN

The sciences and industries that are involved in this effort are multiple and varied, including labs and companies engaged in computer engineering, genetics, robotics, information sciences, and nanotechnology. These currents of development, which are moving just below the surface of our culture, are beginning to erode some of our most basic assumptions pertaining to the human body and its ability to engage with its environmental context. Though the epicenter of this shift lies in the biotechnological advancement of the human body, these changes are re-informing our relationship to our bodies not only biologically and technically, but also culturally.[22]

The human eye didn't work any differently as our knowledge of optics advanced through the centuries, but architecture certainly took cues from each of these advancements in understanding how geometries and space were perceived. This goes as far back as the use of entasis in early Greek columns, a technique that increased the diameter of the column around its lower third to correct an optical illusion that would otherwise make the column appear concave—thought to be a weakness in human visual perception. Francesco Borromini created a forced-perspective arcade in Palazzo Spada (1632) that took advantage of current developments in optic knowledge, including new instruments for constructing those perspectives.[23] Thus, each of these increases in awareness about the body simultaneously gave us access to our surroundings in new ways. As our sensory perceptions increase and expand, so do the potentials of our architecture. Architects direct that new knowledge into materials, technologies, and representational techniques, and their work has defined historical eras in terms of the relationship of the body to its environment (from concepts of smooth space to deconstructivism, modernism, the Baroque, and so on). Yet until now, information about the body for the most part was something to be discovered, not invented.

Techniques for bringing a human body back from injury or debilitation so it can work the way it did prior to an accident or ailment will soon provide abilities that exceed the patient's abilities before the injury or illness. The hearing implants for the child born with a hearing defect will be more sensitive than his or her parents' ears. Will we choose to refrain from making our eyes sharper than those we were born with? Or do we tip the scale ever so slightly, cross that line, and exceed that which has been determined as average eyesight? When ideal levels of sensory perception exceed what has been collectively determined as average at birth, the context in which we live will be under pressure to accommodate desire for that heightened perception, and the human body and its environment will enter into a new relationship—not of accommodating each other, but of racing to outpace one another. This new relationship demands a reciprocal design process, one that negotiates between what architects are able to control and deploy in the environments humans move through and what the body can sense. After all, if the way people perceive their environments is changing, shouldn't the constructs and territories designers make evolve as well?

The result is a type of arms race between the capacities of material energies and the human body's ability to perceive them. The physiology of the human body has been seen as constant within architecture, but as we begin to perceive additional informational energy that was thought previously to be undetectable to the body, the architect will gain control over new architectural shapes and spatial organizations. Architecture no longer needs to be reflexive to knowledge learned about the body; it can now precipitate the body's development! This eclipses the trajectory to date of translating knowledge about the body into environmental constructions, and instead offers a projection of new environments and materials that demand the particular advancement that the body needs to better engage them. Neither the environment nor the human body is seen as accommodating the other, but instead the two are intertwined. If neither is seen as static, then one cannot be understood as a datum. As we've seen, not only are the materials and stimuli in the environment malleable and capable of being redefined, but our nervous systems and brains are also plastic. Given architecture's long history of importing contemporary scientific discoveries to re-inform its production, the architect is in the best position to direct such a convergence and intersection of the body and the changing environments around it. Architecture can do more than nest within the world it sits in. It's the vehicle for negotiating and reinterpreting the world we intend to perceive.

1 V. G. Dether, *The Physiology of Insect Senses* (Bungay, Suffolk, UK: Chapman and Hall Science Paperbacks, 1971), 1.

2 Jakob von Uexkull, *A Foray into the Worlds of Animal and Humans, With a Theory of Meaning*, trans. Joseph D. O'Neal (Minneapolis: University of Minnesota Press, 2010), 43.

3 David B. Dusenbery, *Sensory Ecology: How Organisms Acquire and Respond to Information* (New York: W. H. Freeman, 1992), 39.

4 Dether, *Physiology of Insect Senses*, 3.

5 Richard A. Kasschau, *Psychology: Exploring Behavior*, 2nd ed. (Englewood Cliffs, NJ: Pearson Prentice Hall, 1985), 187.

6 Ibid.

7 David Howe, ed., *Empire of the Senses, The Sensual Culture Reader* (New York: Berg Publishing, 2005), 6.

8 Dominique Janicaud, *The Human Condition*, ON series (New York: Routledge, 2005), 1.

9 Brendan Maher, "Poll Results: Look Who's Doping," *Nature* (2008), http://www.nature.com/news/2008/080409/full/452674a.html (accessed 25 October 2012).

10 Such predictions and the research labs and engineers advancing them are many. Juan Enriquez postulates the next step of human evolution to be an artificially bioengineered trajectory called Homo Evolutis.

11 S. M. Breedlove, M. R. Rosenzweig, and N. V. Watson, *Biological Psychology*, 6th ed. (Sunderland, MA: Sinauer Associates, 2010), 215.

12 Howard C. Hughes, *Sensory Exotica: A World beyond Human Experience* (Cambridge, MA: MIT Press, 2001), 153.

13 Dusenbery, *Sensory Ecology*, 121.

14 Constance Classen, "McLuhan in the Rainforest: The Sensory Worlds of Oral Cultures," in *Empire of the Senses, The Sensual Culture Reader*, ed. David Howe (New York: Berg Publishing, 2005), 148.

15 Lisa Cartwright and Brian Goldfarb, "On the Subject of Neural and Sensory Prosthetics," in *The Prosthetic Impulse: From a Posthuman Present to a Biocultural Future*, ed. Marquard Smith and Joanne Morra (Cambridge, MA: MIT Press, 2007), 125.

16 Quinn Norton, "a Sixth Sense for a Wired World," *Wired* (June 2006), http://www.wired.com/gadgets/mods/news/2006/06/71087?currentPage=all (accessed 6 May 2013).

17 Hughes, *Sensory Exotica*, 204.

18 Norton, "a Sixth Sense for a Wired World."

19 Dusenbery, *Sensory Ecology*, 282.

20 Kevin Warwick, "Upgrading Humans via Implants—Why Not?" *Interdisciplinary Studies in the Long Nineteenth Century*, No. 7, *Minds, Bodies, Machines*, guest edited by Deirdre Coleman and Hilary Fraser (2008), 7, www.19.bbk.ac.uk (accessed date), Center for Computing in the Humanities, King's College London.

21 Ibid.

22 Janicaud, *The Human Condition*, 1.

23 Kim H. Veltman, "Perspective and the Scope of Optics" (unpublished paper, Toronto, 1992), http://www.sumscorp.com/img/file/1992_Perspective_and_the_Scope_of_Optics.pdf (accessed 24 October 2012).

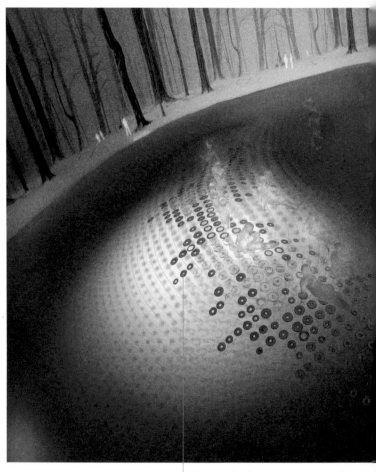

The mound and seating areas engage the body beyond the ergonomics of sitting and reclining. Enhancing the existing energy systems in the environment makes spaces habitable that would otherwise be thought unusable during the late fall and winter months of Chicago.

The project's shape, as perceived by a visitor, is determined not only by the mound, but also by the characteristics of the contrasting microclimates nested within the courtyard, made visible in Chicago's often snow- and ice-covered winter streetscapes.

SIRENUSE, 2011
Model / Rendering
Sean Lally WEATHERS

The boundary edge of the space can be held tightly as the air moves out from the source below and into the environment above. Air temperature, velocity, and the release of particulates into the air join together to inform the spatial boundary edge.

Spatial boundaries can be both visually detected from a distance as well as sensed through tactile means, triggered by thermal and electrical charges and the resistance of air particulates that the human body comes in contact with as it approaches and enters the spaces.

PROOF 001, 2013
Model / Rendering
Sean Lally WEATHERS

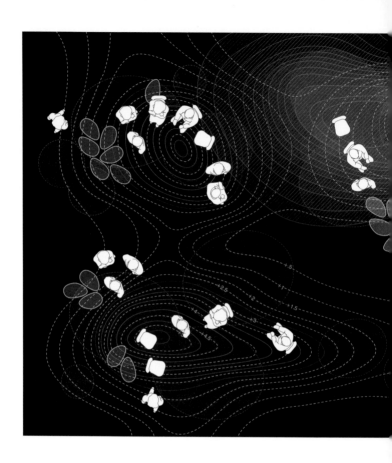

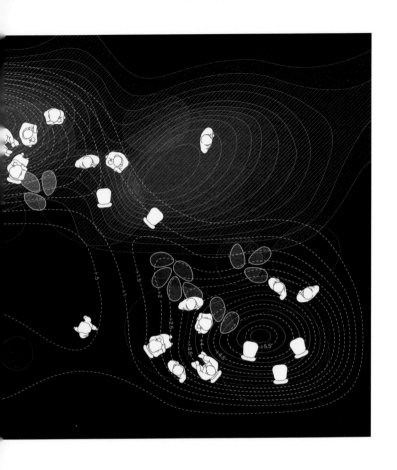

UNDERTOW, 2009–2010
Site Plan
Sean Lally WEATHERS

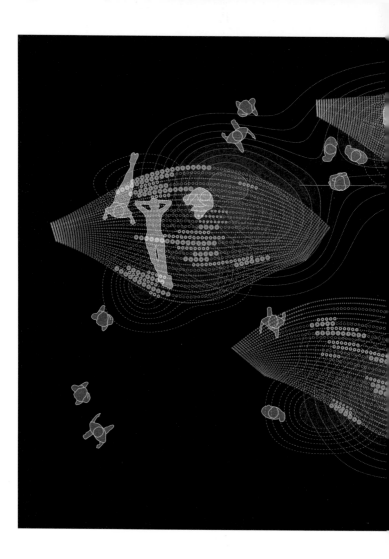

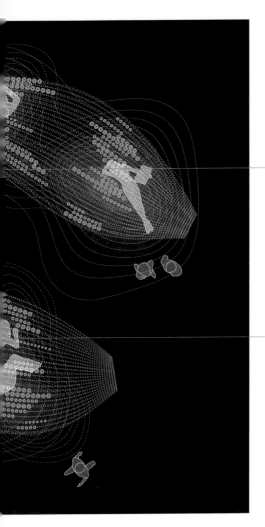

The individual segments of Shagg, tied to ergonomics and the spatial nodes created by the material energies, are not always coincident with one another, sometimes spilling out between the carpet sources or overlapping to produce intensified zones.

Noise cancellation, thermal conduction, and blue-enriched light production layer together to produce multiple spatial zones of varying intensities and individual microclimate pockets.

SHAGG, 2009–2010
Site Plan
Sean Lally WEATHERS

The new spaces are perceivable not only through the seating shapes, but also in the vegetative growth of the warmed soil and in the clustering of individuals around the seats.

The change in color of the
figures represents the human
body's engagement of the
material energies defining
the space.

WANDERINGS, 2008–2010
Rendering
Sean Lally WEATHERS

THROUGH THE LOOKING GLASS

Julius Shulman's photographs are best known for the lifestyles staged within them, most notably in the Case Study Houses of Southern California—specifically his photograph of Case Study House #22 by Pierre Koenig (the Stahl House). In removing the surfaces from this photo, the intention is to look to how *material energies* can conceivably inform not only the shapes and forms of architecture, but also the social setting and interactions that take place within. Our intuition tells us that the social engagements and lifestyles seen in the original photograph will not remain the same, no matter how hard one tries to reproduce them with material energies. The proclivities of the material energies will inevitably affect the spatial and social hierarchies in place. Tinkering with such a fundamental aspect of architecture (the material properties of our physical boundaries) can best be played out through "scenario building"—seeking to question and re-inform the spatial and organizational consequences as we embrace the unique characteristics of material energies. This means more than swapping one material for another; it is a realization that such a fundamental shift in our strategies— from defining space by mediating the surrounding material context to engaging and designing that context itself—will inform our assumptions about existing activities and social dynamics.

FIRE COLUMN

Yves Klein's *Fire Column* is a starting point for defining
material energies as building blocks for architectural construction.
The material energies here sit within a new progression of
symbolic column orders and have their own proclivities and
material properties that inform architectural shape and aesthetics.
Just as classical columns exhibit proportional relationships
tied to the human body's shape and sensory perception (most
notably optics and entasis), so will *material energies* reflect
the growing knowledge of the human body, and the aesthetics
and shapes of the architecture these materials produce.

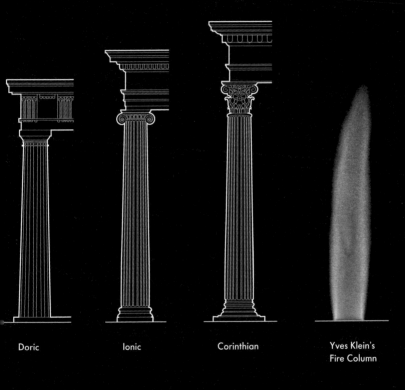

Doric   Ionic   Corinthian   Yves Klein's
                                             Fire Column

SHAPE SUCCESSION

The physical properties of the boundaries that define this architecture are tied to the relationship between the intensity of the *material energies* used and the climatic variables of the surrounding context exerting pressure on those qualities. As the properties of the climatic surroundings fluctuate (increasing in humidity or wind speed, or dropping in temperature), the architectural shape must respond by either intensifying or decreasing the energy output needed to maintain the specified series of boundaries for refining and organizing a given space. Additional energy can be exerted to offset external forces and maintain a desired geographic control, or the boundary can be allowed to withdraw from the area or even go dormant. This feedback relationship between the material energies and the existing climatic variables influences aesthetic as well as physical boundaries and the spatial control of the architectural shape. Like a campfire, the flames can increase in size to offset the increasing cold, wind, or darkness of the site and therefore maintain the geographical desired edge, but this means the intensified flames are burning hotter and brighter in the center, changing the architecture's physical and aesthetic properties in the process.

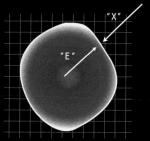

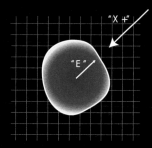

"E" is the generation of material energies. "X" designates the existing energies of the site (climatic and existing site factors). The interaction between "E" and "X" informs the shape of architecture.

When "E" remains constant and "X" increases, the geographic boundary will decrease.

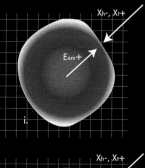

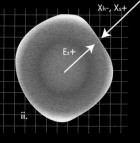

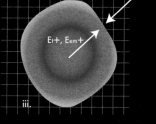

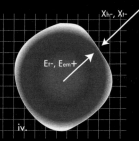

In order to maintain the physical edges of the architectural shape, a continuing feedback relationship between "E" and "X" must be maintained. This continued and varied interaction of energy between {Et, Eem, Es, Ec} ⊂ E and {Xh Xt, Xl, ...} ⊂ X will result in aesthetic variability.

WHERE PROGRAM BOXES GO TO DIE

Program boxes made of foam blocks are the ultimate abstraction of how the geometries of solid materials are used to structure and organize architecture. These boxes often stand in for the itemized components needed to create more complex wholes (apartments, parking, a lobby, circulation), which are stacked and arranged into a larger architectural form (an apartment complex)—represented in the "stacked duck." Another version of this same approach can be seen when architectural form is determined by massing out the overall outer profile of the building. The overall form is then subdivided into individual territories, as a butcher would outline the cuts of meat in a cartoon of an animal's carcass—giving us the "stuffed pig." Realizing how our ingrained techniques for representing space are bound by lines, surfaces, and blocks helps us to question and seek other avenues for exploring spatial organizations. This is the death of program boxes.

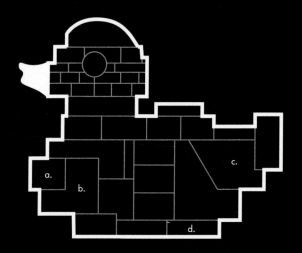

STACKED DUCK

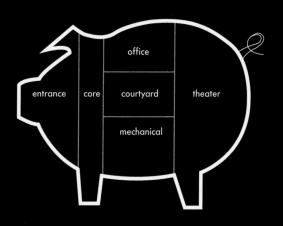

STUFFED PIG

GRADIENT NOLLI

If we were to map our cities today, showing not the walls and envelopes, but rather the artificially conditioned, climate-controlled (primarily interior) spaces versus the unconditioned (exterior) context, we would see as striking a dichotomy of figure-ground as we see in Nolli's eighteenth-century map. When we look at the city not as public versus private space, but as conditioned versus unconditioned space, the surfaces and geometries of architecture are often coincident with and responsible for fortifying these boundaries. Yet as cities vent their infrastructure exhaust, as buildings release energy dumps from their mechanical systems, and as air-conditioning spills from commercial spaces onto streets and plazas, it becomes apparent that this dichotomy is less clear—the boundaries have become blurred and temporal, requiring a gradient reading and mapping of our spaces and activities. Currently, many of these conditions are unintentional by-products. Yet within them lies the potential for architects to take a proactive approach to designing with these energy fallouts. Gradient climate zones originate from these buildings, growing and shrinking with seasonal changes. These gradient "parks" shift in size and intensity, often spilling out and connecting with each other in milder seasons, while shrinking and acting as disparate entities in the more extreme winter months.

PUBLIC AND PRIVATE SPACES (EXCERPT)
Giambattista Nolli's 1748 map of Rome

CONDITIONED AND UNCONDITIONED SPACE
(heated, cooled, and / or tempered against sound)
Contemporary mapping of Rome

MONSTERS IN ARCHITECTURE
(A FAMILY PORTRAIT)

The author Stanislaw Lem, best known for his 1961 science fiction novel *Solaris*, was critical of the American science fiction scene during the mid-1970s: he believed that the genre was increasingly used for making ever scarier monsters in film and writing, when it should have been used to address more difficult topics, including social and political concerns. Known as the "Lem affair," the controversy that resulted from his comments would lead the Science Fiction Writers of America to revoke his honorary membership in 1976. The architectural profession's fascination with surfaces and geometry during the design process has culminated in the production of its own monsters, while it has largely neglected conversations about how alternate forms might question existing spatial or organizational systems. These monsters can appear unique at the skin level, but the anatomy below (typologies of courtyard, double-loaded corridors, stacked floor slabs) remains unchallenged. A profession that has witnessed technological advancements in software visualization and fabrication has been caught up—making scarier monsters by manipulating surface treatments—but has rarely questioned the changing worlds and environments they might be living in.

Jet Jaguar   Softwarian   Godzilla   Megalon   Parasiteian   Gigan

THE SHAPE
OF ENERGY

Shape conveys the edges and boundaries of a system. This might be through a form of representation on paper or through a physical edge that can be experienced in person. Shape not only transmits to an audience the existence of these boundaries, but also provides a medium on which one can place value, whether aesthetic or monetary. The physical properties of the materials that architects use influence the physical configurations, conglomerations and subdivisions, and identifiable boundaries of architecture. The proclivities of material energies can go on to influence larger spatial typologies and social experiences. But before these material energies can be witnessed or embraced by architecture, they must first be given shape.

Understanding the importance of being able to give shape to architecture through the materials that architects build with might appear to be so fundamental as to require no clarification. Yet, this understanding is precisely what has been evading the architect when it comes to working with energy. If an individual were asked to identify the shapes of energy in architecture today, he or she would point in the direction of the technologies that harness energy (photovoltaic cells, wind turbines, generators) or the devices that release it (heating, ventilation, and air-conditioning [HVAC] systems and light fixtures). This is because energy innovation is recognized today only in the technologies and devices associated with its collection and release, not in what architects do with the energy *after* it is released. Working in direct collusion with the technologies and devices that harness and release energy are the surface geometries of architecture that bind the energy inside; energy fills the interior cavity of an existing architectural form like air going into a car tire. The devices of energy collection and release, coupled with the armatures of mediation (surfaces), are thus the sole means today for defining the shapes given to architecture. All attention, aesthetics, and value have been placed on the mechanisms that control energies, and have been turned away from the energies themselves, on the assumption that shape and value cannot be respectively achieved and absorbed anywhere else. The ability to give architectural shape to energy is of primary importance in advancing future energy research within architecture and beyond, yet it appears to be one of the most elusive aspects of this current project.

In order to glimpse architecture's fundamental shapes, it is necessary to strip away the layers of surfaces and devices that have been built on top of the very energy systems that support nearly any given activity in the first place. Putting aside the ergo-

FIRE COLUMNS
Yves Klein's *Fire Column*.

nomics associated with furniture and the body, it is the control of energy systems (acoustics, light levels, humidity, air velocity, and heat or cold) that is required to maintain human health and comfort, and to protect goods and valuables from extreme climatic conditions. By not giving shape to the energy systems themselves that are at the core of our social experiences, we fail to see architecture's most intrinsic characteristics. These characteristics instead are being perceived through the restraining filters and signifiers believed to be the sole way to instill value in architecture. Looking to energy as a material not only provides another medium for absorbing aesthetics and monetary value, but also gives architects the opportunity to contemplate and observe the as-yet-unknown spatial and organizational ramifications of using material energy systems with their own distinct proclivities. It is through these material energies that the true shape of architecture can be found, at present buried beneath and obfuscated by surface and shells, mechanisms that have for so long been assumed to be the architect's only option for designing and maintaining the physical boundaries and spaces that hold our public and private events within them.

Moving from points, lines, and surfaces to gradients of intensities and fallouts is bound to have novel spatial and organizational implications for daily activities and lifestyles as architects explore strategies for dealing with these new shapes. The physical properties of material energies will influence our core understanding of how a geographic edge condition is defined, how these edges behave, how apertures and paths for circulation are created, and how those spaces conglomerate and subdivide. Therefore, this discussion of shape as it pertains to energy involves much more than simply replacing one material system (solid matter) with another (material energies).

What begins as a conversation about the properties of material energies and the shapes they are capable of producing eventually opens up to include larger typologies, as more diverse organizational systems of circulation and density are required to accommodate more complex activities and programs. The intention in this chapter is first to better understand the characteristics and proclivities of the architectural shape of energy before seeking to draw out its spatial and organizational implications for activities and social experiences. The chapter will show in detail that architectural shape is more than the properties of the materials used to define a geographic space; it is instead the combined result of those material biases intertwined with the social pressures and forces placed upon the activities they seek to facilitate.

CHARACTERISTICS OF AMPLIFIED ARCHITECTURE'S SHAPE
Feedbacks

When energy is released, whether heat and light from a burning piece of wood, sound waves from a speaker, light from a flashlight, or steam from a hot cup of coffee, that energy seeks to dissipate into its surroundings. "Energy spontaneously disperses from being localized to becoming spread out if it is not hindered from doing so," states the second law of thermodynamics. The rate at which that energy spreads is based on the parameters of its surroundings, including existing temperature, light levels, humidity, and air velocity, to name a few. For this reason, the shape of an architecture made of energy cannot have an unwavering and consistent form; instead, it manifests the continuous feedback that occurs between the energy exerted to create a physical space and the context of atmospheric conditions that interact with that energy. Here architectural shape is formed by a boundary that represents a relationship between material energies and existing climatic conditions. These two factors interact in ways that influence not only the architecture's initial shape, but also the degree to which that shape can fluctuate and vary over time as external atmospheric conditions change. Architectural shape will therefore always be in a feedback loop between the existing environment and the energy system an architect produces. This feedback goes beyond the external forces acting upon its shape to include those that enter the architecture itself. An "energy balance equation" emerges in which anything that crosses that boundary (such as, additional people, including their body temperature, physical mass, or supporting objects) affects the energy system (as in the architecture).

The material energies' shape has the inherent potential to shift in size or resolution, moving among an array of other physical attributes, from one moment to another, because its climatic context is variable and interacts with the energies that make up the intended shape. The same street light produces what the eye perceives to be a different boundary edge under a full moon compared to that under a new moon, when less light is reflected back to Earth. The distance between the light source and the ground does not change—the size of the circle of light on the ground remains the same—but the edge between the area of light on the ground and the darkness beyond will appear blurred and less defined when more light is reaching Earth's surface and being reflected from surrounding surfaces than on a darker night without a full moon. The same effect can be observed when using a flashlight outside during the evening's transition from dusk to nightfall. The definition of the boundaries that a particular light is able to produce will increase as the sun sets lower. The darker the surroundings, the more defined the flashlight beam's edge will become. The boundaries of material energies, and therefore an architecture defined by such properties, are not isolated closed systems standing in opposition to their contexts (as in the case of solid construction and surface mediation strategies), but are instead open systems, arrangements informed by the ever changing relationship between an architectural system and its environment.

This does not mean that the material control required to hold a spatial boundary—so a living room or office space, for example, can be used whenever needed—will necessarily waver as surrounding atmospheric variables or the "energy balance equation" changes, but it does mean that additional energy might need to be exerted or released to maintain such a configuration. This might very well affect other aesthetic characteristics of the architectural shape.

Actual Color May Vary
Neither campfires nor street lighting can be expected to maintain a continuous boundary edge during varied climatic and seasonal conditions if the heat or light emitted from them remains constant. In a campfire, more wood can be added as fuel to increase the size of the flame in order to offset additional cold, wind, or

darkness at the site and therefore maintain the desired geographical edge. When the external variables of ambient light, humidity, air particles, wind, and thermal conditions change, a specified boundary will either grow or shrink because those external variables exert influence on the energy source creating the boundary. Additional energy can then be exerted to offset those external forces and maintain a desired geographic control, or the material energy can be allowed to withdraw and go dormant, like a street light turning off until it is needed once again. Adding energy produces further changes. As you place more wood on a fire to overcome the cold, the flame burns hotter and brighter, and the color of that flame itself might very well change slightly. The decision to maintain the thermal boundary around the fire as the surrounding climate pushes against it, which requires an increase in fuel, thus has an influence on the aesthetic qualities of the fire.

As the external physical properties of the surroundings fluctuate, architecture produced through amplification of material energies must intensify or abate to maintain the specified series of boundaries needed for organizing spaces. This increase or decrease of intensity will manifest itself through other characteristics of the architecture, particularly the aesthetics of the architecture's shape. A campfire is the most simplistic example, but it serves to illustrate the basic principle clearly for all forms of architectural boundaries created from energy. These boundaries will always have a dialogue with the context that they exist within because both consist of the same material properties.

But this increase in energy intensity is not a proportional progression, just as increasing the length of a cantilever by twenty percent does not necessarily mean that the new overhang will require the same percentage increase in materials and structural depth: the energy in the increased cantilever will instead be stored in the solid masses used in the structure. However, in the case of material energies, the additional deployment of energy to offset external forces from the surrounding environment will be seen or felt within the physical characteristics of the boundary edges. In the case of maintaining steady heat from a campfire, the flame gets larger, brighter, and warmer in the center, re-informing its aesthetic characteristics in order to maintain the specific physical boundary and area of warmth.

This fluctuation might occur from one minute to another, seasonally, or over decades as climatic variables change and as other nearby design projects or constructions influence the particular system. What this produces in architecture is a unique relationship between the ability to define and hold the physical boundaries that permit a specific activity or event to occur within it, and the ability to maintain a particular set of aesthetic characteristics, a relationship in which the aesthetics could certainly change if the physical boundaries are upheld. A fluctuating relationship in an architectural shape between aesthetics and spatial boundaries differs rather substantially from what is associated with architectural form now, which is thought to be static and unwavering with aesthetic qualities generally inscribed into the solid boundaries produced.

Tracers and Tactile Shapes
Shape is not predetermined for recognition solely by the eye. The spectrum of a material energy's properties sometimes extends well beyond the realm of what is visible to the human

eye today. Therefore, the shape of energy in architecture might take on other characteristics beyond the visible spectrum, detectable through other sensory perceptions or because they influence secondary or tertiary systems that the eyes might be able to see.

Where does a campfire start and end? More specifically, can you define the edge that separates the heat and light that the campfire delivers from the surrounding environmental context of ambient air temperature and light that already exists there? Is it that edge where you can see the light dissipating into the darker surroundings, or is it the thermal boundary your body can feel as you determine which location is most accommodating for sitting by the fire? What about the edges of a magnetic field, or a frequency of sound, or a thermal condition without a visible indicator—flickering flames, for example? The human eye can't perceive heat, but an exhaust grate releasing heat on a swatch of land during the winter will produce a visible patch of growing green grass surrounded by snow. This shows that the temperature is unique to a given location. You can't see humidity levels either, but you can see condensation when air on one side of a window is colder than on the other side, as the air on the warmer side will hold more water and condense on the cold glass. It follows that invisible energy sources used for boundaries might require a tracer to run in parallel, to give us the indicators that fit with our predominant senses, like the scent tracers the gas industry places inside natural gas to alert the general public to its existence in the case of a leak. The tracers used to track the velocities of a river current's flow patterns below the surface are another example.

Being able to identify the boundaries of these energy systems at any particular moment is important because those edges (once they are tightly controlled as an architectural material) will come to define architectural space and will therefore require a shape that designers can articulate abstractly, through various representation techniques, and that inhabitants can identify, through their occupation and use of the architecture. It also raises the question of how architects can communicate such an architectural shape to an audience prior to its delivery. The relationship between a representation used to convey design intentions and what can be expected in a final deliverable when working with materials that are not always visible to the human eye and are inherently fluctuating is difficult to manage. Yet it is of critical importance. What is required is an ability to design and convey the specified bandwidth of change that is expected in this architecture's shape. Tracers coupled with the new activities that are made possible on a given site may help alleviate these issues. However, the tolerances associated with final dimensions, the assembly of materials, and those finishes used to judge the success of a project's final completion as it goes from design on paper into construction will certainly take on a slightly different meaning.

Tolerances

Our control over material energies is not definitive, like our control over geometry. Tolerances in geometries as they relate to solid construction are expressed in fractions of an inch or millimeters, both in the required specifications for constructing a final product and in the drawings conveying design intentions to a future audience. Conveying an image of an architecture's shape so that it can be recognized and commodified is no small task with regards to energy systems, yet it is of considerable importance; not only does shape communicate intentions to a wider audience, but it also acts as a means of refining architectural intentions during the design phase.

Furthermore, being able to plan for these much larger tolerances requires knowledge not only of the material energies deployed, but also of the activities a project requires and the atmospheric variables associated with the specific geographic locale in which the project will be situated. In some regards, this geographic locale plays a type of vernacular role in the production of this architecture, as the architecture's performative abilities, shapes, and organizational systems will most certainly be related to its climatic context. The existing climatic variables of a site will influence the shape of the architecture, whether that site is at a particular latitude or in a particular microclimate within a city.

As a simple example: if you pick a house from a catalog that is made of wood framing, steel, glass, or any number of other construction systems, its shape will be the same in Guadalajara, Mexico, as in Boston or Seattle (assuming the same precision of construction). Your energy bills may vary, but the house's shape in terms of spatial control—size of rooms, circulation, and even color—will not. In contrast, the shape of a given project produced through the amplification of material energies will be strongly informed by the relationship between the material energies used in its construction and the feedback from the existing atmospheric variables unique to each region and site (whether Guadalajara, Boston, or Seattle). This does not mean that a similar design intention and strategy cannot be deployed across these three climates when designing a house, but it does mean that certain qualities, as well as potential organizational implications, will vary from one site to another, making a singular, sellable image of the house difficult to devise.

Unlike the catalog house with a reproducible image that can be built nearly anywhere due to standardized assembly processes and building materials like wood, steel, and paint, architecture through amplification produces a type of micro-vernacular shape as each site creates a unique feedback relationship to the energy systems deployed. Seasonal variability in humidity levels, temperature, and winds might be a regional characteristic of a city that architects are aware of, but even the microclimates that make one site unique from another three blocks away will inform and play a role in the project's shape. These differences yield a vernacular shape that transcends its predecessors, which are tied directly to the surfaces and walls that mediate their surroundings, and which include the porches and overhangs of homes of the southern United States before air-conditioning, or the massive walls of adobe structures in the Southwest, to name just a few. The vernaculars generated by material energies, in contrast, have their own characteristics.

SHAPE SUCCESSION

With a better understanding of the proclivities associated with the material energies that inform this architectural shape, we can turn our attention to the social and organizational implications that are sure to emerge as notions of stasis and architectural boundaries are reframed. As noted earlier, the feedback relationship between the material energies that form a given architectural space and the climatic variables of its context produces a shape that differs greatly from what is traditionally associated with architecture. This approach to shape, however, does coincide with currently changing characterizations of how environmental systems and ecosystems demarcate and define geographic locales. Perceptions of ecological systems have evolved substantially over the last century. Ecosystems were once thought of as closed systems, seeking a state of equilibrium with predictable end states, but they are now thought of as dynamic and nonlinear, where "disturbance is a frequent, intrinsic characteristic."[1] Our growing understanding of ecosystems and the boundaries utilized to define them now recognizes that diverse pockets have the possibility of multiple outcomes with no determined final condition. An architecture in which shape is constructed by amplifying and harnessing shared contextual materialities can learn something from this change in thought.

Robert E. Cook in his essay "Do Landscapes Learn?" describes what he believes is a paradigm shift in how we think about ecologies and their changing characteristics over time, referred to as ecological succession. *Succession* is a term roughly a century old that explains the process through which an ecological community changes its configuration. This configuration is defined as the combined relationship of variables within a system of vegetation, fauna, and microclimates, including the chemical compositions of air and soil, that change from one geographic locale to another and that separate one ecosystem from another. Ecosystems are discernible from one another by observing these combined, often subtle, individual changes, which form discrete territories that can be demarcated along geographic boundaries.

What separates earlier views about the development of a particular ecosystem—let's say a stable deciduous forest—from how scientists see this process today is the belief in what is referred to as a "climax community." This is a model in which succession is believed to stop when a system arrives at a state of equilibrium. In the absence of any major disturbance, it was believed that such an ecosystem would persist indefinitely, with this end point (equilibrium) being the climax. Should that particular deciduous forest burn, the model predicted that after the fire it would seek once again to reach the climax community of plant, animal, and insect life that existed prior to the fire. However, research has shown that events that alter an ecosystem's makeup are not only frequent, but also go on to inform that changing ecosystem's future characteristics.[2] Previously considered highly predictable, succession has instead been shown to be highly contingent on the "history" of an ecosystem and its surrounding context—the local conditions and events that place pressure upon it, including changes introduced by human culture.[3] Succession under these circumstances may display multiple possible pathways as well as multiple end states, "assuming that any end state is ever reached."[4] The characteristics of an ecosystem's shape (the geographic boundaries it defines, and the properties of its plant material, soil, and air) are not understood to be constant, but instead vary over time.

This concept of succession and a climax community undoubtedly resonates with traditional notions of architectural form made of geometries and solid construction, as both are predicated on a closed system. We strive to protect a building (from earthquakes, hurricanes, fires, and decay, for example), but we view its form (from initial representations to its construction and occupation) as a singular, pinnacle condition. When that form eventually fails and succumbs to one of these forces, whether earthquake or decay, it will leave behind artifacts that others can use in an attempt to piece together and so identify the lost climax state, replacing it in what we all consciously know to be a process of continuing succession (i.e., history). It almost goes without saying, however, that the building material that defined that climax state was never in a closed system. Everyone can recall watching a building succumb to the elements around it over time, eventually being absorbed into the advancing and changing environments, whether due to natural conditions (fire, hurricane, decay) or political ones (demolition). But as a working state of architecture, the building's usability is contingent on perpetuating this climax state for as long as possible. When that climax state can no longer be held, it quickly falls into what is characterized as "decline" until it can be repaired back to its climax state. Very little variation beyond these two stark poles is acceptable.

To fortify this notion, building materials for architecture have advanced in the pursuit of strength and durability against the variables around them that might degrade the climax state that the architect envisions. To maintain this unyielding aesthetic or formal configuration, builders have sought out construction technologies and materials that produce forms through trapped and ossified energy, marching forward from bundled grasses to wood, stone, iron, steel, glass, and plastics, all in an attempt to enforce a designed and unwavering climax state against the depredations of the environment it is set within. These material advancements have created greater territorial control in terms of construction precision, increasing a design's longevity by allowing it to outlast a growing list of external forces while also inscribing within it our exact aesthetic desires. When projects like the Guggenheim in New York, the Louvre in Paris, or the landscape gardens of Thomas Church or Garrett Eckbo are completed, they each exist with no visions other than their continued "as is" condition, both in terms of territorial control and aesthetic value. The value of a project's form in these cases is judged on its ability to maintain the singular configuration originally envisioned and later recognized by all those who have seen it in image or in person. These projects are considered "preserved" as long as they maintain these same characteristics through time.

The idea that architecture exists as a closed system comes from a very clear and logical place. Architecture has a responsibility to secure and facilitate a wide range of activities (from outdoor restaurant dining to a hospital operating room), many of which cannot vary in their organizational configurations or exist without some steady measure of protection from outside forces. This, of course, is what makes architecture distinct from environmental ecologies. It is this need to meet the requirements of activities and social experiences beyond what an existing site might be able to offer prior to the architect's intervention that makes a given shape architecture. A theatrical performance, gallery opening, or your ability to entertain in your own living room is not thought to be subject to the weather. Your guests' ability to arrive at the event may be impeded by variables of rain or wind, but the staging of the event itself is not. Those programmatic activities are not thought of as being in repose or on hold.

An architectural shape consisting of material energies is made of the same materiality as the surrounding context, which makes the production of a historical artifact more difficult, but which also makes that shape more flexible, able to accommodate the shifting demands of changing activities, expansion, and recession. This flexibility is an embedded characteristic that can be held as tightly or nimbly as one chooses. Decisions can be made to reinforce an organizational system against any one of a range of external forces on an hourly, seasonally, or yearly basis.

So how do we reconcile this ingrained association of desirable stasis in architecture (climax state)—the demand to strictly maintain a building's image and its defined spatial control—with what is ultimately a fluid and variable feedback relationship between material energies and their climatic context? The first thing to do is recognize that with material energies the shape's aesthetic value will become variable along a determined bandwidth as long as the shape maintains a spatial and organizational specificity. Or vice versa: a shape could maintain aesthetic criteria while letting spatial configurations ebb. Architects can manage this ever-changing balance through an approach called "shape succession."

Shape succession is a way to embrace the intrinsic characteristics of the material energies that construct an architectural shape while simultaneously addressing the need to secure the parameters of social activities occupying that shape. What is desired is a shape that is capable of holding those boundaries when needed, but is also potentially able to release that grip if other opportunities to organize space are pursued. The question of whether material energies can facilitate the needs of architecture is less in doubt if architects and the individuals using a space are willing to recognize and accept a shifting notion of stasis, if not in terms of the geographic boundaries of that space at a given moment, then certainly in terms of their aesthetic qualities. This produces an architectural aesthetic that varies in some regard as the material energies attempt to maintain the properties of a defined and desired spatial boundary by changing in order to overcome the influence of external variables acting upon them.

SHAPING SOCIAL EXPERIENCES

The boundaries constructed within an environment influence behavior both directly, by physically interacting with the body, as well as culturally, through constructed social norms. Solid architectural boundaries carry physical implications that cause difficulty to the body should one try to question them, including dealing with the social responses of those who witness such behavior. Try and walk through the drywall partition in front of you or test the glass wall of the office building you're in and see what the response is, both from your own body and from the people around you. The physical properties of the boundary, as well as the actions available to the body in responding to it, create an understood datum related to both the property of the material and how our bodies sense it, as in what happens if the body were to come in contact with it.

A concrete wall will provide greater security and privacy than a glass wall, but it won't allow the same engagement between two people on either side of it. A short picket fence will demarcate the edge of a house's property, prevent (most) family dogs from escaping, and simultaneously make it clear to passers-by where trespassing begins, all while never obscuring views in to or out of the property. The articulation of boundary edges as they are defined and interpreted for construction in architecture comprises an objective reality, in the process producing a datum of control. These datums of control may be overruled by a particular individual's mischievousness or by the confusion of cultural norms: a room with a door, two windows, seating, and a great video projector and sound system may be prescribed as a lecture room, for example, but this doesn't prevent someone from running through the door and out one of the windows at any given

MATERIALS AND
SPATIAL BOUNDARIES
Ground Plan by Rahel
Hegnauer.

point. But two rooms connected by a single corridor certainly prescribe the path for that individual prior to coming through that door and exiting out the window. To put it another way, the physical boundaries that are created, predicated on our body's ability to perceive and interact with the properties of those boundaries, dictate our interactions with each other and the bounded space. It's not always possible to know how a space will be used, but by working with the physical properties of the boundaries that structure and organize architecture, a dialogue can be created between the possible actions of people and the characteristics of the spaces defined.

Architectural shape is more than the manipulation of materials alone. It comes from a dialogue between the physical boundaries architects create to organize people and goods, and the larger social trends tied to economics, politics, philosophy, and communication that originate outside the purview of architecture. Each applies pressure upon the other in ways ultimately unknown until they come into direct contact, at which point they begin to influence and re-inform one another. The physical boundaries that architects define and then subdivide, conglomerate, and connect together so as to manage complex social interactions (schools, public libraries) or highly specified activities (theaters, hospitals) influence the very nature of those activities initially specified. Pairing the characteristics and opportunities of shape with the social demands outside of architecture is how spatial typologies come about.

Discussions of shape may begin with the properties of the materials that construct it or the ways it can foster a single chosen activity, but it is through outside social pressures and the need for larger and more complex organizational strategies that architectural shape really emerges. Understanding the proclivities of a material system beyond the construction of a singular space, and how that system might inform larger typologies and organizations, is what is most intriguing in architecture and yet most difficult to predict. These results may be intentional, while in other cases the implications may trickle down and play out over longer stretches of time in unexpected and unplanned ways. As they become apparent in hindsight, these typologies can be made available for deployment once again through revisions and refinements in future design. As Louis Pasteur said, "In the field of observation, chance favors only the prepared mind."[5] It is therefore only by identifying two variables simultaneously—the proclivities of materials and the larger social trends that inform architectural shape—that architects can be prepared to recognize the opportunities stemming from this dialogue, which they can then exploit or suppress in creating architecture's shape.

Robin Evans reminds us that architecture is more than a practicality, and that the shape and configurations it takes are never "neutral translations of such prerequisites." The configurations of the rooms, systems of circulation, and visual connectivities that surround us appear so common that we forget the significance these configurations have had in defining our social dynamics and lifestyles; we fail to remember that these configurations and typologies have an "origin."[6] The assumption that certain configurations of spaces and typologies within our daily lives are simple and "ordinary" is a delusion, because they in fact develop from dozens, if not hundreds, of iterations of this dialogue, and in turn go on to influence our social lives.[7]

The example that Robin Evans points to that most clearly illustrates this dialogue is what he refers to as the yet-unwritten history of the corridor. This typology of organizing a building's activity and layout appears to be so ordinary and obvious to architect and inhabitant alike that it is assumed to lack a history, even though it has given shape to countless architectures. In truth, the corridor is thought to have originated in the last few years of the sixteenth century in John Thorpe's Beaufort House in Chelsea, England, where it is notated on the plan as "a longe Entry through all."[8] Prior to the introduction of the corridor, rooms existed in a matrix; each room contained multiple doors, making it necessary to pass through one room to reach another. This movement would obviously disturb the activities in those rooms as individuals passed through. The corridor provided the opportunity for people to move along a shared pathway connected to each of the rooms, simultaneously separating the activities within those rooms from the circulation of individuals looking to access a separate space.

The matrix configuration of rooms that existed prior to the seventeenth century treated the human body in domestic spaces much differently than the corridor would in the nineteenth century. Where the matrix of rooms reinforced the overlap and intersection of bodies passing each other in space, the corridor reinforced their separation. Much of this shift can be attributed to the changing notion of what the *interior* was.[9] Specifically in England, the notion of the interior underwent significant changes between the late fifteenth century (just prior to the emergence of Robin Evans's example of the corridor) and the mid-nineteenth century. The late fifteenth century defined the interior as one's inner spirituality, separated from the outside world. The eighteenth century would see "interiority" more as "inner character and a sense of individual subjectivity."[10] In the nineteenth century, it would come to mean the inside of a building or room, a notion that emerged with the significance of a private, physical, three-dimensional space.[11] The hermetic effect produced in isolating rooms from one another reinforced the separation of physical bodies that was rooted in this changing psychological notion of the interior. As the notion of the interior grew to concern more than the individual body, the need to separate that body from other bodies also grew more acute. Material manifestations of the interior, including room and corridor planning for the mid-nineteenth-century house, did more than just articulate this change. Over the course of those hundred-plus years, the articulation of space and movement in architecture was in dialogue with an ongoing change in individual subjectivity, and these two factors would influence social engagements, interactions, circulation, and aesthetics in those interior spaces.

The example above is but one of many that illustrate that material change and fabrication alone are not responsible for the spatial typologies and shapes of architecture that emerge over time. It also serves to highlight that it takes a tuning of the proclivities of the materialities afforded us at any particular moment with the social pressures of economics, communication, politics, and the like, to bring us novel organizational systems and architectural shapes. But if architects fail to observe these two variables in dialogue, questioning both so as to speculate on the potential spatial and organizational implications at play, they will fail to do anything more than mimic and reproduce existing and known organizational systems. Regardless of the novelty of any new forms they might design, they will be only imitating existing typologies. Giving shape to an architecture of material energies is a means to avoid the passive aspects of designing that begin by defining activities and then constructing boundaries to facilitate them.[12]

The underlying agenda within this book is to point the reader toward the new spatial typologies that could develop from these material energies and to suggest possibilities for how they might influence new social experiences. But in truth, the best we can do at the moment is to bookend the discussion by identifying the characteristics of material energy systems on one end and current social trends on the other. In between there will be iterations upon iterations by multiple voices observing and looking for opportunities to strengthen and re-inform both ends of the poles. The development of this architecture's shape requires attention to selected social trends and a willingness to embellish both the dialogue among those trends and the proclivities of the material energies that facilitate them. Over time, architects will recognize these new organizational techniques as a means for facilitating social standards and producing architectural typologies. It is unlikely that the shapes and norms of architecture we might instinctively dismiss as neutral and ordinary were produced by singular decrees and immediate manifestations, but instead they developed by amplifying the existing currents that course below the surface of architecture, requiring multiple iterations to rise to the top. A dialogue among multiple architects produces these typologies gradually until they are exemplified by several individuals or traced back to a few earlier projects through the recognizable elements of now-ubiquitous shapes. The architecture of mediation developed through many voices and has taken on many titles over the course of successive movements through history (classical, Gothic, Renaissance, Baroque, modern, postmodern). The hope is that an architecture designed by amplifying environmental energy systems will encourage just as many voices to take part in its manifestation, once again not through a singular directive but through a multiplicity of efforts.

One implication is certain: the continuous advancement of material energies in architecture will produce a material system (energy) that leaves much less of a trace of our activities than the materiality that came before it. Petrified energy in the form of blocks of stone and beams of steel leaves evidence behind for centuries as artifacts of fallen "climax states," but material energies dissipate almost immediately, leaving little behind—like turning a light switch off and on, material energies are quickly gone but easily brought back. The building blocks of material energies attain entropy more quickly than those of traditional construction, dissolving and dissipating their shapes when no longer attended to. The resultant architecture might appear almost to dissipate on command when the localized energy is permitted to spread out.

This description may portray them as more frail, but material energies might also be seen as more nimble. Unlike a climax state, which projects past accomplishments long into future decades, this architectural system is more fleeting and therefore more adaptable to change (climatic, economic, social, and aesthetic), offering a shape that could prove far more valuable in times of rapid change. Shape succession looks to what some might point to as an architecture constructed of an energy system's greatest weakness and suggests that very weakness as its greatest attribute. One day people may reflect back on their memories of today's artifacts of monumental and ossified energy blocks and see them as cold-blooded dinosaurs that existed prior to the warm-blooded architectures that by then move underneath their feet. Shape succession creates an architecture that is more agile and has an innate ability to be upgraded. The properties of material energies that require them to be continually active and perpetually reproduced to define edges and boundaries also work to meet an ever-growing demand for immediate updates, rapid changes in spatial needs, and continued advancements in performance simulations. Because material energies produce an architecture that is continually being regenerated, its forms are easily enhanced and fine-tuned. Imagine an architectural shape (including its aesthetics and the intensity of its boundary control) that is continuously replenishable. The ability to renew both quickly and continuously throughout a project's lifespan seems pertinent today. The shapes might be entropic, but the social implications of these organizational opportunities and social experiences might be longer lived. This is a very different type of artifact for architecture to leave behind.

These characteristics of an architectural shape are tied to more than the properties of the material energies that construct them. As the Robin Evans examples demonstrate, the shapes of architecture are simultaneously influenced by both materials and cultural and social pressures, with the latter imprinted on the former, which are themselves reshaped by the ongoing dialogue between them. Though the full implications of these new architectural shapes are still to be discovered, we are aware of the proclivities of its materiality and now need only to engage further in a dialogue with today's evolving social demands. The results are new shapes of architecture.

1 Robert E. Cook, "Do Landscapes Learn? Ecology's 'New Paradigm' and Design in Landscape Architecture," in *Environmentalism and Landscape Architecture*, ed. Michel Conan (Washington, DC: Dumbarton Oaks, 2000), 120.

2 Ibid., 130.

3 Ibid., 121.

4 Ibid.

5 L. Pasteur, Speech delivered at Douai on December 7, 1854 on the occasion of his formal inauguration to the Faculty of Letters of Douai and the Faculty of Sciences of Lille, reprinted in: Pasteur Vallery-Radot, ed., *Oeuvres de Pasteur* (Paris, France: Masson and Co., 1939), vol. 7, 131.

6 Robin Evans, "Figures, Doors, and Passages," in *Translations from Drawing to Building and Other Essays* (Cambridge, MA: MIT Press, 1997), 56.

7 Ibid., 89.

8 Ibid., 70.

9 Ibid., 88.

10 Charles Rice, *The Emergence of the Interior, Architecture, Modernity, Domesticity* (London and New York: Routledge, 2007), 2.

11 Ibid.

12 Rem Koolhaas and Bernard Tschumi, "2 architects, 10 questions on program," eds. Amanda Reeser Lawrence and Ashley Schafer, *Praxis: Journal of Writing and Building* 8 (2006), 6–15.

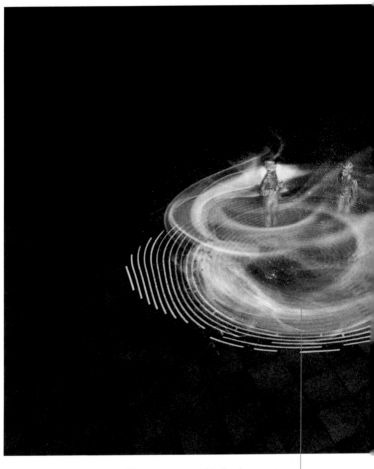

The energy mass within the plaza creates a
physical shape and space usable during
Chicago's winter months. The shape of the
space can be tuned in intensity to accommodate changing recreational and public
programming needs and can even go dormant
when not needed.

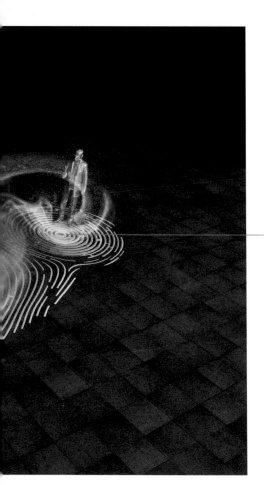

Embedded into the existing stone paving of the plaza, the project sits flush on grade. Two openings are covered with a porous, walkable surface. The larger opening pushes air out and launches it on a circular course before it is pulled back down and recycled by the smaller opening to the rear.

PROOF 001, 2013
Model / Rendering
Sean Lally WEATHERS

The single ground plane has multiple discrete spaces that can be occupied and experienced as intense microclimates, each with a designated diameter, occasionally with one nested in another.

Vegetation (algae, lichen) is contained within silicone pods nestled underfoot. The bloom and rate of growth of the vegetation are controlled with varying blue and red light spectra, as well as through the vegetation's placement in a particular microclimatic zone.

UNDERTOW, 2009–2010
Model / Rendering
Sean Lally WEATHERS

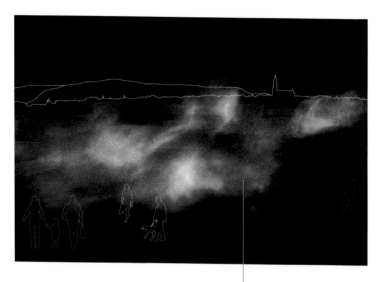

The visual characteristics of the "climatic wash" come from not only the juxtaposition of growing vegetation against the surrounding snow-covered grounds in winter but also the interaction and energy transfers between these locally produced microclimates nested within the existing larger climatic trends of the city.

VATNSMYRI URBAN PLANNING, 2007
Rendering
Sean Lally WEATHERS

KAOHSIUNG MARINE CULTURE & POP MUSIC CENTER, 2010
Models
Sean Lally WEATHERS

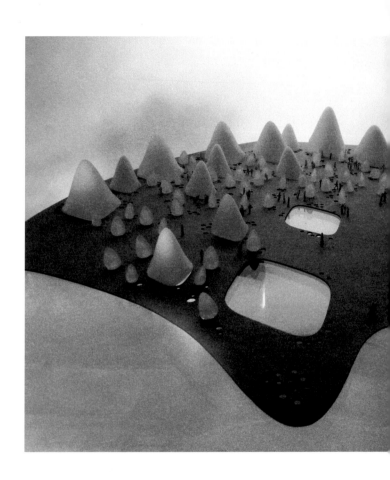

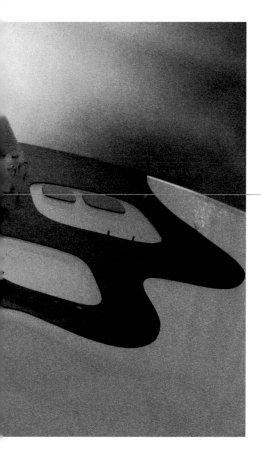

The museum and exhibition portion of the twelve-hectare site is splintered into poche-like segments that hold the most valuable parts of the program, those for display and storage. Each is a discrete pocket located within a larger architectural shape made from a range of material energies, providing entrance points, a lobby, and visitor circulation that are spatially and aesthetically distinguished from the larger site.

KAOHSIUNG MARINE CULTURE & POP MUSIC CENTER, 2010
Model
Sean Lally WEATHERS

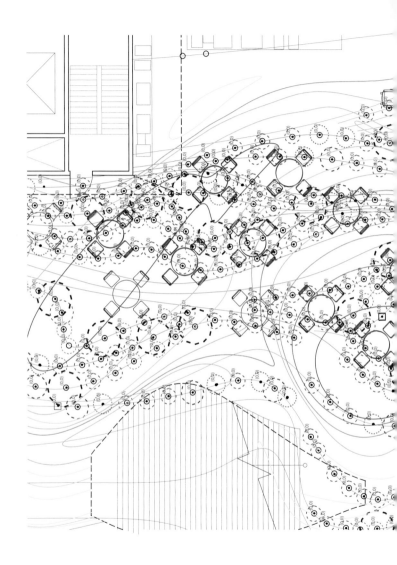

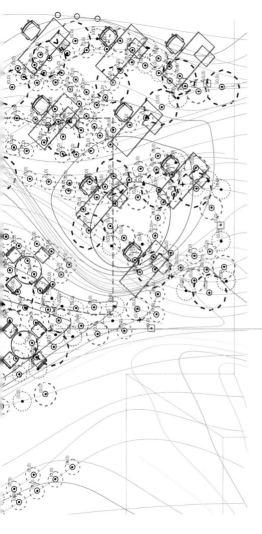

Interactions and exchanges between the material energies (thermal exchanges, pressure changes) that maintain specified activities produce distinct boundary types and gradient edges that define access and location within these "interior" spaces and encourage circulation paths to develop.

CHELTENHAM MUSEUM ADDITION, 2007
First Floor Plan
Sean Lally WEATHERS

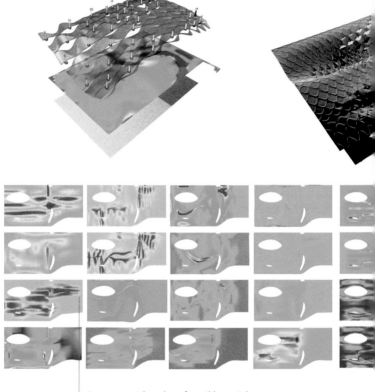

An exponential number of possible spatial opportunities exist internally, based on where the material energies are released and controlled, all while the home maintains the single, static geometric form that is used to deploy them. These latent spatial conditions are available to be called on for the varied needs of domestic living.

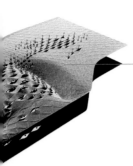

The network of 300 interconnected points, which include air handlers, requires air flow and its gradient temperature to pass through varied formal configurations and into the space beyond. Though the geometric form stays static, the spatial boundaries created by the material energies are flexible and varied.

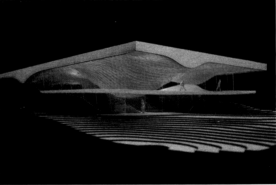

SIM HOUSE, 2006
Renderings, Model
Sean Lally WEATHERS

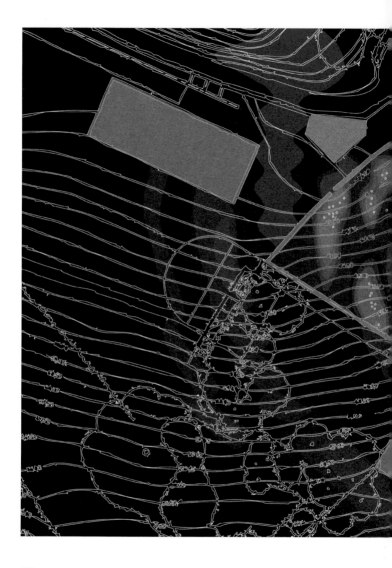

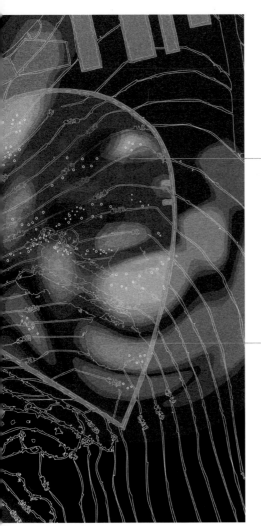

Surrounded by an existing perimeter wall, the project proposal seeks to create a garden of multiple and discrete world climates without the glass partitions generally associated with greenhouses.

Creating these multiple climate zones is an attempt not only to produce recognized climates (tropical, dry, moderate, continental, polar), but also to explore the artificial intersections produced when these zones are defined and held in close proximity.

HADSPEN PARABOLA, 2007
Site Plan
Sean Lally WEATHERS

APPENDIX

PROJECT CREDITS

PROOF 001
Chicago, Illinois, USA
2013
Installation proposal
Design Team: Sean Lally WEATHERS
(Evgeniya Plotnikova, Maged Guerguis)

SIRENUSE
Chicago, Illinois, USA
2011
Installation proposal
Design Team: Sean Lally WEATHERS
(Thomas Kelley)

GDANSK MUSEUM OF WORLD
WAR II
Gdansk, Poland
2010
Two-stage competition
Design Team:
Sean Lally WEATHERS
(Federico Cavazos, Marina Nicollier,
Matt Vander Ploeg)
and OOS AG (Christoph Kellenberger,
Christiane Agreiter)
Environmental Design Consultants: Atelier
Ten

KAOHSIUNG MARINE CULTURE &
POP MUSIC CENTER
Kaohsiung, Taiwan
2010
Competition
Design Team: Sean Lally WEATHERS
(Matt Vander Ploeg)

SHAGG
San Fernando, California, USA
2009–2010
Installation proposal
Design Team: Sean Lally WEATHERS
(Marina Nicollier, Matt Vander Ploeg)

UNDERTOW
2009–2010
Installation
Design Team: Sean Lally WEATHERS
(Lauren Turner)

SITUATE
Perth, Australia
2009
Two-stage competition
Design Team: Sean Lally WEATHERS
(Marina Nicollier, Stephen Coorlas)
Environmental Design Consultants:
Atelier Ten

HOMETTA
2009
Private residence
Design Team: Sean Lally WEATHERS
(Brian Shepherdson)

WANDERINGS
Variable geographic locations
2008–2010
Installation/research
Design Team: Sean Lally WEATHERS
(Benson Gillespie, Ned Dodington, Brian
Shepherdson, Curt Gambetta, Viktor
Ramos)

TAMULA LAKESIDE
Võru, Estonia
2008
Two-stage competition
Design Team: Sean Lally WEATHERS
(Viktor Ramos, Marina Nicollier)
Executive Architect: Morris Architects,
Houston

ESTONIAN ACADEMY OF ARTS
Tallinn, Estonia
2008
Two-stage competition
Design Team: Sean Lally WEATHERS
(Viktor Ramos, Marina Nicollier, John Carr,
Ali Naghdali)
Executive Architect: Morris Architects,
Houston

MATERIALS AND APPLICATIONS
Los Angeles, California, USA
2007
Proposal
Design Team: Sean Lally WEATHERS

AMPLIFICATION
Los Angeles, California, USA
2006–2007
Installation as part of the Gen(h)ome
Project (2006)
Curated by Open Source Architecture,
Kimberli Meyer, and Peter Noever;
The MAK Center of Art and Architecture
Design Team: Sean Lally WEATHERS
(Andrew Corrigan, Maria Gabriela Flores)

CHELTENHAM MUSEUM
ADDITION
Cheltenham, England
2007
One-stage competition
Design Team: Sean Lally WEATHERS

VATNSMYRI URBAN PLANNING
Reykjavik, Iceland
2007
One-stage competition
Design Team: Sean Lally WEATHERS
(Andrew Corrigan, Paul Kweton)

HADSPEN PARABOLA
London, England
2007
Two-stage competition
Design Team: Sean Lally WEATHERS

ASPLUND LIBRARY
Stockholm, Sweden
2006
Competition
Design Team: Sean Lally WEATHERS

SIM HOUSE
Houston, Texas, USA
2006
Private residence
Design Team: Sean Lally WEATHERS

S.I.V. HOUSE
Variable geographic locations
2006
Research proposal
Design Team: Sean Lally WEATHERS

ABOUT THE AUTHOR

SEAN LALLY, 1974, is the founder of Sean Lally WEATHERS and an assistant professor at the University of Illinois at Chicago.

ACKNOWLEDGMENTS

I want to take a moment to acknowledge that any form of success embedded in this publication is rooted in the friendships and family I have around me. I've been fortunate to be able to call many of the people I work with friends first. Thanks to the Chicago Clan I was lucky to stumble into and the eternal relationships originating in Monmouth County. A majority of this book was written while I was in Rome, and I'd like to say thank you to both the American Academy in Rome for the unique opportunities they provided as well as the School of Architecture at the University of Illinois at Chicago for helping me stay there. Thanks to the Graham Foundation for the Advanced Studies in the Fine Arts for their financial support, to Kim Hibben for help with image permissions during the final stretch, and to Jayne Kelley and Polly Koch for your insights on the manuscript.

THE AIR FROM OTHER PLANETS

Conceived and written by Sean Lally

Design: Sean Lally and Integral Lars Müller/
Esther Butterworth
Copyediting: Polly Koch
Proofreading: Laura McLardy
Lithography: Ast & Fischer, Wabern
Printing and binding: Kösel,
Altusried-Krugzell, Germany
Paper: LuxoArt Samt, 135 g/m^2

Lars Müller Publishers
Zürich, Switzerland
www.lars-mueller-publishers.com

ISBN 978-3-03778-393-1

Printed in Germany

The book is supported by
the Graham Foundation for Advanced
Studies in the Fine Arts.

GRAHAM FOUNDATION

Dedicado a Marina, el corazón de todo.